A Journey through Unexpected Grief

Theresa Rosati Sanson, R.N.

Quixote Publications

Quixote Publications
490 Merrimak Drive
Berea, Ohio 44017-2241

10 9 8 7 6 5 4 3 2 1

Library of Congress Cataloging-in-Publication Data

Sanson, Theresa Rosati, 1959–
    A journey through unexpected grief / Theresa Rosati Sanson.
        p. cm.
    ISBN 0-9677583-6-X
    1. Grief. 2. Bereavement--Psychological aspects. 3. Brothers--Death--
Psychological aspects. Loss (Psychology) I. Title.

BF575.G7 S36 2001
155.9'37--dc21   2001048695

Cover photo: Vanessa Sidoti
Author photo: Edward Mulvenna

Contents

Introduction

     Journal entries are indicated with a * throughout.

Dedication

In loving memory of my Louie
For the joy, the laughter, and the love we shared
and in memory of Grandma Toon, Grandpa, Aunt Anita, and
Ashley

Dedicated to
Mom and Dad
Marie, Anita, and Joe, my siblings
Alice—for helping me to begin this journey
Colleen—for believing in me when I didn't believe in myself
Mary—who inspired me to keep writing when I didn't think
I had anything left in me to write about
Michelle—for being my earthly guardian angel
Vanessa—for sharing your beautiful photo for the cover
My sons, Tony and Mike, for their patience and understand-
ing when Mom wasn't quite Mom
To my loving husband Tony—for being the driving force be-
hind me. When he showed an inkling of doubt that I would
ever finish this book, I had to prove him wrong.
Last, but never least, to God Almighty, for with him all things
are possible.

Publisher's Note

On a snowy night in March 2001, I finished the initial edit of Theresa Sanson's manuscript for this book. "Some worthy advice here," I thought, reaffirming my decision to publish her book. Having only experienced the loss of my parents, who lived long and happy lives, I could not fully relate to the shock of unexpected death that Theresa described. Yet I recognized that she shared her feelings with a compelling poignancy and intensity.

What a difference a few hours can make. By midmorning of the very next day, my dear husband had died suddenly. I found I was truly walking the same path of sorrow as Theresa had. Now I was engulfed in that numbing pain, that hollow emptiness.

Several months passed before Theresa's book was scheduled for production. When I resumed work on it, I realized that I understood many of the feelings I had been experiencing and that I had been using some of the same comfort measures she suggested for alleviating grief. Her book had evidently made a profound impression upon my subconscious and helped to set me on the road to healing.

I feel privileged in helping to bring Theresa's message to others.

Patricia M. Mote, Publisher
Quixote Publications

Introduction

Probably like yours, my life has been filled with ups and downs. My general attitude has been to take things as they come, one day at a time. Until one day when it happened—a loved one died unexpectedly, and my life was turned upside down and inside out. I had no idea how to turn my life right side up again. I did not know how to change things back to normal. I wasn't even sure what normal was any longer. I doubted that my life would ever return to normal again. I doubted I'd ever be able to smile, laugh, or feel joy in my heart again. I was clueless as to how to pick up the pieces of my life and begin to put them back together. I didn't know where to start and doubted I'd find the energy to accomplish this monumental task.

Through this experience I've learned that grief can be personal with the loss of a loved one or universal as with the death of Princess Diana. Grief is not selective to age, race, gender, nationality, or religious beliefs. Grief can happen when you least expect it. It can attack you like a mugger in the middle of the night or sneak up on you like the fog rolling over the ocean. Grief can be heart-wrenching, energy-draining, complex, and multifaceted. I've attempted to throw out the complexity of grief and put it into basics.

I would like to invite you on my journey and share with you the events that brought this grief to my life. Then I will share the actual journal entries of my feelings, as the events were happening, and stories that touched or changed my life.

Finally, I'll share the things I did to help me on this most difficult journey—how I began to put my life into order again and move forward when I didn't think it was possible. I thought that the rest of my life would be filled with sorrow and pain, that I would only be able to survive and function from day to day, and that I would never learn to live again.

You may think it is not possible to live again, but it is. You can look grief straight in the eye, and you can conquer it. Grief may try to strip you of everything, but you can beat it. Begin with an open mind and see where the journey takes you. I welcome you on my journey through unexpected grief.

T.R.S.

1
Ashley's Story

My journey begins with Ashley, a nine-year-old girl with cancer, a patient at Cleveland's Rainbow Babies and Childrens Hospital. She had leukemia and had contracted aspergillos, bacteria of the brain and lung. Someone whose immune system is intact could shake it off, but for someone with an immune system that's compromised, it can be deadly.

She had multiple complications. Her family would walk in and out of her room and down the hall, and occasionally I'd say "Okay, everyone in a single file line." We'd laugh, for some reason they would exit her room in that order. She had been on the floor about three months, and I had never taken care of her. In some ways I was relieved, since she had so many complications. I was concerned that I didn't have enough knowledge and skill to care for her properly.

One day, it happened. I got to work for my shift and Ashley was assigned to me. I asked the day nurse to tell me about her and expressed my concern since I'd never taken care of her before. The nurse gave me a full report and told me, "Terri, you'll be fine. It's not that bad." I thought she might be in better hands with a more experienced hem-onc (hematology-oncology) nurse, but we had a few complicated cases on the floor, and the patients needed to be divided equally. So I thought, "Terri, she's yours for eight hours. You can do it." I went through all the charts of my patients and headed to Ashley's room. I introduced myself and told her I'd be her nurse. She said, "Okay," and those big, beautiful blue eyes sparkled. That's all it took. I was hooked. My skills, knowledge, and mother instincts took over, and if anything was new for me, I asked a more experienced R.N. for help.

I liked to do little extras when my female patients felt well enough. I'd bring them videos, give French manicures, or use colored polish with a variety of decals or rhinestones. I can't honestly remember if we did a manicure the first night (I think we did). Once we started, we did Ashley's nails and other little girls' every weekend that I worked.

Almost each weekend that I worked, Ashley was my patient, but on the few occasions that she wasn't, we still did her nails. If I didn't have time during the shift, I'd stay after to do her nails. At times the other nurses would tell me that on my occasional weekend off, if Ashley's nails were chipped, she'd say, "Terri is off this weekend. I'll have to wait until next weekend."

Ashley had gorgeous nails, and she loved to have a French manicure. The last time I did her nails, she had picked out the various colors and decals. I asked her if she was sure she wanted them done that way because it was an awful lot for one set of little hands. She said that she was sure, and when I finished her nails, she didn't like them. My initial thought was "Well, we can do them next time," but I didn't say that. Instead, I told her to remove it with the polish remover.

Ashley had never done that before, but we started all over again. I think some of it was related to the medication she was on. We had started her BMT (bone marrow transplant) protocol. She was such a pleasant child. As ill as she was, she'd always try to smile or have a kind thing to say. She continually thought of others. The last day I took care of her she asked if we could make up the chair bed. She would sleep in it that night so that her mom could sleep in her bed and get a better night's rest. Taking care of Ashley was a privilege and an honor. Getting to know her family was a pleasure—Mary, her mom, Mike, her dad, and Jordan, her brother. Mary is a truly wonderful person, filled with kindness, compassion, and sensitivity. It's easy to see where Ashley's example came from.

I had a weekend off, and as I drove to work on July 20, 1996, I was looking forward to seeing Ashley. I had made a copy of a tape for her and had forgotten to bring it, so I took the original from my car. If she liked it, I'd bring the copy in next week. As I was walking down the hall, I looked for the nameplates on the wall, and I didn't see Ashley's. At first, I thought she got moved back to her old room, but her nameplate wasn't there either. I thought she must be in the PICU (Pediatric Intensive Care Unit), because it's not uncommon after a BMT to be in PICU for a time.

When I got to the desk, I asked, "Where is Ashley, in PICU?" Before they even spoke, I could tell by the looks on the two night nurses' faces that something was wrong.

"Oh, God, Terri, you don't know." But I knew then.

"Know what?" I said.

"Ashley died last week." I couldn't believe no one had called me. They knew how special she was to me.

I asked, "What happened?"

"She just starting going downhill before the BMT. She ended up in PICU on a ventilator."

My heart sank. Ashley was gone. I went into the back room to compose myself. I still had a whole shift to work yet. That's why we always try to call the nurses of patients that die. That way you have the time you need at home to get yourself together.

I got through the weekend, and that Monday night I called Mary, Ashley's mom, to give my condolences and to see how they were doing. As expected, they were trying to keep busy and taking one day at a time. We talked for a while, and I shared with Mary how concerned I was the first time I took care of Ashley and how much her child had touched my heart. She made me feel wonderful by some of the things she shared, and this reinforced for me that I'm accomplishing what I've set out to do by being a nurse. She said that a handful of other nurses and I had been so helpful. She shared that on Wednesday July 10, 1996. Ashley had been asleep and had been moaning. Mary thought she was in pain, so she inquired, and Ashley told her she was in no pain but was having the most beautiful dream about angels, and the same thing had happened later when one of the doctors had inquired about her being in pain. She said that Ashley had gone peacefully.

Ashley loved Garth Brooks. One of her therapists wrote and told him how much Ashley loved him. Garth sent her a personal letter saying that when he came to Ohio, he wanted to meet her. Along with the letter he sent a T-shirt, CDs, and other Garth memorabilia. Garth will never know the joy he brought to this little girl. She was so thrilled. She was always listening to his music and her other favorite country artists.

I shared with Mary that "In this profession I always try to keep a professional distance from patients and family, so if the outcome is less than what we'd hope for, it hurts less." But with Ashley it was different. Ashley will always be in my heart. Mary shared that she'd never forget me, and I told her that I felt the same way about her family. She asked if I wanted a picture of

Ashley, and I reminded her that I had one. What had touched me in such a special way was that Mary said she had Ashley's nails manicured, polished, and rhinestones put on in honor of me, because I had been the one who had taken the time to do this with her. I truly felt honored.

Ashley's death was difficult; other patients on our floor had died, and it hurt, but I had let Ashley into my heart. I think it will be a long time before I let that happen again. I give all my patients my best when I'm caring for them, but I try to keep a reasonable distance. I'm always professional, but sometimes I don't have a choice as to who touches my heart and who doesn't. After all, I am only human.

Had I known Ashley had died, I would have gone to the funeral, which is another thing I usually don't do. But Ashley was different; sometimes the rules change. Since I wasn't at the funeral, Mary said it dawned on her on the way home and she said to Mike that I probably didn't know. She was right.

Going to work was difficult after Ashley died. She was one of the reasons I enjoyed being at work so much, and she brought so much joy to me. There will never be another Ashley, but I'll continue to care for my patients to the best of my ability. I know that's what Ashley would want and expect from me, and after all, I wouldn't want to disappoint one of God's little angels.

2
Louie's Story

I t was a beautiful July day in 1996. Everything was right in our family. Mom was doing well; she had made it through the six-month period after her open heart surgery, and that evening we were all going to a family wedding. The wedding was beautiful, and we were lucky. We had parents that had been together for forty-five years; we had celebrated that milestone in June. My two sisters, two brothers, and I were all in good marriages, had healthy children, and we were all very close and loved each other. What more could one ask for in life?

Everyone looked terrific in fancy attire. We laughed, danced, and had a great time. As the evening drew to a close, we kissed, hugged, and said our goodbyes until next time. All was right in the world. We were blessed...or were we? I never imagined that would be the last time I'd see one of my family members alive.

The call came at work, that third day of August. My husband Tony said I needed to get to the hospital. Louie, my brother, was in critical condition. Doctors suspected a heart attack. A heart attack? But he was only forty. I made arrangements for the other nurses to take my patients. I had to get to the hospital, now, but how? It was over an hour away. I called my sisters at work, knowing they'd want to go with me to the hospital. The adrenaline had already started pulsating through my body.

Someone suggested that I call the hospital before I headed out, because that particular hospital would not be able to deal with a critical heart patient. Louie would be transferred out to the Cleveland Clinic. I took her advice and called. After I was transferred two or three times, a nursing supervisor came on the phone. I told her who I was, why I was calling, inquired about Louie's condition, and if there would be time for me to pick up my parents. Without any warning, she said, "I'm sorry to tell you, your brother just died." I dropped the phone, slid down the counter to the ground, and let out a sound I didn't think a voice could make. Two of my peers helped me up, and then I remember sitting at a table in our back room crying. They had to be mistaken. It couldn't be true. Louie couldn't have died, not from a heart attack, not at forty. I just saw him a couple of weeks before. He was fine. He looked as handsome as ever—that salt-and-pepper hair, those beautiful, chocolate brown eyes. He died. It couldn't be.

I wasn't expecting this; it came out of nowhere. Initially, there was no pain; my brain was trying to comprehend what the body and heart had already understood. At the same time, my heart was trying to encircle itself into a protective shell so as not to break completely in half. My body went into a type of functional shock. I had to get to my parents, especially my mother. I had to call my sister-in-law Debi. Was she alone when it happened? Was she with him? The details were so evasive. I was told he was in a video store when he felt sick, began having chest pain, asked for help, and fell over. Bystanders had started CPR until the paramedics arrived. I had to do something. Sitting at this table crying wasn't helping anyone.

The others didn't want me to drive, but I had to. Too much time was passing, I needed to gain control of this uncontrollable situation. Besides, my attempts to reach my sister-in-law were futile. I headed out to pick up my sisters, Marie and Anita, but when I got on the road, I couldn't remember how to get to where they work, so I called Tony from the car phone, crying. He calmed me and told me how to get there. A short time later he called me back and said to go straight to my parents' house. My sisters would meet me there.

I headed to Mom's. The ride seemed endless. Why was traffic so heavy? My mind was racing in so many directions—to Mom, to the children, to my best friend Colleen. I had to reach her, but she wasn't home. I've got to call Debi; maybe she is home by now. Dial the number, it's ringing, the machine kicks on. Oh, God no, it's Louie's voice. Hang up the phone. No, no, no. What was I thinking? Why had I called his house? My body begins to tremble; my head and voice keep repeating No, no, no! I've got to get to Mom.

I finally arrive at my parents'. Mom was sitting on the couch. The physical appearance was Mom, but the eyes didn't look like her; she was obviously in shock. I went to her crying, taking her in my arms. No reaction. My fears have come true. My touch, my voice isn't going to help, not this time, at least not at this moment. What should I do next? Time passed slowly. Family and friends began to arrive.

The phone rang. Anita's sister-in-law, Sandy, answered. It was Anita. Sandy didn't want Anita to hear her voice shaking, so she handed me the phone. Anita began asking all sorts of questions. I told her just to get to Mom's. She said, "I know he's dead, Theresa. Just tell me." I told her he wasn't, just to get to Mom's.

She started shouting, "If you took me out of work for nothing—I know something is wrong. Just tell me. He's dead, isn't he?"

I'm not really sure how long we attempted to debate this, but when I told her he had gone home to Jesus, she started crying into the phone. Anita later told me she heard Mom in the background, sobbing. That's how she knew.

I tried speaking calmly in an attempt to calm her down, and got the location of where she was on the road. I told her to pull off to the side, that I would come and get her. I didn't want her driving like this. She began to calm down and said she didn't want to because Marie was behind her and she didn't want her to know what was going on, not yet. God, what was wrong with me? Why did I tell her? I should have been stronger and just let her yell until she got to Mom's. She is still ten or fifteen minutes away. Why didn't I just tell her the hospital was transferring him to the Clinic, and we were all going to drive there together. My brain isn't working. What if something happens to my sister, too, because of my stupidity? Please, somebody, wake me up. Let me out of this nightmare I'm having.

Our cousin Jerry and I got in the car and drove to where Anita was and followed Marie and her back to Mom's. Anita ended up in someone's arms, and I ran out to Marie. I didn't even have to say the words. She knew, as the tears streamed down our faces, and we embraced. Slowly, we all headed into the house.

Mom continued to come in and out of her shock-like state. She begged me to take her to the hospital to see Louie. Mom's sister, Aunt Chris, added, "You have to. Don't deny her this." Oh, God, I'm not sure if I can do this. I can't be the strong one this time. I feel as if I'm dying inside. No, no. Be strong. You have to do this for the sake of your family, what's left of it. My heart and my head would do some very serious battles.

All of the necessary arrangements were made, after a very

frustrating conversation with the day nursing supervisor. I called and asked how long Louie's body would be at the hospital before the funeral home would be picking him up. (I didn't know he would go for an autopsy, since he hadn't died in the hospital and because of his young age). I explained to the supervisor that my parents wanted to come to the hospital. She told me in a matter-of-fact tone that the body was in the morgue. I told her in no uncertain terms that I would not allow my parents to view my brother's body in the morgue. Where was her compassion?

I asked if she could have his body moved to a more appropriate place. She stated, "Well, I suppose we could move him back to ER, but you do realize we are very busy." My brother is gone, and she's telling me how busy ER is. ER was not what I had in mind, either, especially if they were busy. I asked if she could place the body in a room that wasn't occupied. She replied, "I'll see what I can do" and told me that by the time we arrived at the hospital her shift would be over, and to ask for the evening nursing supervisor. From the way I was feeling and the lack of compassion this woman displayed, dealing with someone else would be for the best. I didn't think I would be able to bear her lack of compassion and our broken hearts all at the same time.

Mom, Dad, Aunt Chris, Jerry, Marie, Anita, my brother Joe, and I headed out in two cars. I don't remember very much of the ride, and the frightening part is that I was driving one of the cars. When we arrived at the hospital, Jerry (our paramedic of the family) suggested I go in first, before the rest of my family. He explained that at times a heart attack victim's appearance can be altered, and I could prepare the family if this were so.

When we went into the hospital through ER, I asked for the evening nursing supervisor. I felt as if everyone was looking at us—hospital staff, security—as if they knew the reason we were there. I'm not sure. Maybe they could tell by the look on our faces. I told Mom to let me go first. She started to get upset and began crying harder, "No, Theresa, you can't stop me from seeing him." In an almost pleading voice I told her that I wasn't going to stop her; I just wanted to go first. Aunt Chris helped calm her.

As we waited for the nurse, my heart and head began to battle. *No, Theresa, you can't—please—I don't want to do this. He's my brother, too. I can't. Please let someone else do it. Please, somebody wake me up.* You must, in case you need to prepare or save the family from further hurt. Come on. Time to be strong. I asked Jerry to come with me. The nursing supervisor, two security officers, Jerry, and I headed down the never-ending corridors. As we were walking, the nurse said how sorry she was for our loss and that she understood; she had also lost a sibling. She then said she had Louie's body placed in the chapel and had special permission to have all the tubes removed before we arrived. She said it would make the viewing of his body a little easier for my parents. This woman was a truly compassionate human being.

When we arrived at the chapel doors, she asked if I was ready. I said, "Yes," but my heart screamed, *No, please don't open the door, somebody please, God be merciful. Wake me up from this nightmare.* As she opened the door, the lights were soft and there he was, lying on the stretcher with a sheet up to his neck and his arms lying at his sides. As I stepped into the chapel, my feet felt like lead. I reeled slightly backwards, and Jerry took hold of me. *Please, don't make me look.* That gorgeous, salt-and-pepper colored hair, but I can't see those chocolate brown eyes; his eyes are closed. Still, he was handsome as ever. I asked the security officer to get my family, to tell them that Louie looked beautiful, and not to make them wait any longer. As my eyes filled up with tears, I kissed him. His body was so cold. *Oh dear God, this nightmare is a reality, my brother Louie is gone. Won't somebody please wake me up?*

The rest of the family began to come towards the chapel with Mom and Dad coming in first. *Okay, Theresa, come on. Time to be strong.* When she entered the chapel, Mom reeled completely backwards. Dad and Jerry or one of the security officers caught her, while the nurse and the other security officer got her into a wheelchair. The pain and anguish on my mother's face was too much to bear. This is too cruel, a mother should not have to go through this. Children are supposed to outlive their parents.

Mom continued to sob as they wheeled her over to Louie. I went up near her, but she was insisting on standing and asking to hold him. I told her that wasn't possible, but she could hug him. As she leaned over his body to embrace him, a tear fell from her cheek onto his, and she said, "Look, Theresa, he's crying." I told her that her tears were falling onto him. He wasn't crying. He was in heaven now with the Lord.

I was overwhelmed with concern for Mom, for Dad, for all of us. How would we survive this? We had just gone through hell and back with almost losing Mom eight months ago with all the heart problems, and here we are again. My body was functioning in a semi-shock mode, going through the motions, doing what had to be done. I don't think I was thinking about the fact that he wasn't coming back to us.

After a short period of time, the rest of my family came into the chapel. I watched to be sure that they would be all right. I didn't want to look. I could hardly bear the pain I was feeling.

How could I bear the pain on their faces too? *My dear God, this can't really be happening,* but it was the whole miserable experience. We were in the middle of this nightmare, and none of us were dreaming. We were back in hell again; at least it felt like it.

After spending time to be sure the family was okay, Jerry and I spoke with members of the code team to find out what had happened. Then Mom, Dad, and I spoke with the doctor in charge of the code. They had done all they could. We all decided to drive to Debi and Louie's house, about a half-hour away. I was beginning to feel physically sick and wasn't sure how long I'd last.

When we arrived, Debi was sitting on the couch. We took turns hugging Debi and the children, as we all cried together. After about a half hour, I felt as if I was going to go over the edge; I needed to get home. Debi had plenty of people to comfort her, and I wasn't sure if I'd make the one-hour and forty-five minute drive home. Jerry and Aunt Chris came with me. I started to drive, thinking it would keep me from being sick, but after about twenty minutes, I just couldn't drive any longer. Jerry took over.

Once I got home, I spent the rest of the night in the bathroom, physically sick, severe nausea, heaving, diarrhea, my body shaking uncontrollably. I was so ill that for a while I forgot why I was sick and what had actually taken place that day. By morning, most of the physical symptoms had eased. I was still nauseous and had a headache, but that wasn't as severe as the emotional feelings I was experiencing—the internal shaking, the bursts of tears—and I still had to tell my boys.

When I felt I had some control of my emotions, Tony and I called our sons, Tony, 13, and Michael, 10, into the living room. As gently as I could, I told the boys I had something very difficult to tell them. We explained that Jesus had decided to call Uncle

Louie home. We told them that it was okay to cry, to ask any questions, and to express what they were feeling. They began to cry. We talked, and Tony and I answered all their questions as best we could.

I knew my physical appearance was a sight, and I was concerned that I might frighten the boys, so I explained, "Mom is having a very difficult time, but I will be all right. It is just going to take some time." I lied. At that moment, I wasn't sure what day it was or how I would begin to put things in order, but I didn't want the boys traumatized any more then they already were.

When I awoke several times during the night, the tears would begin to roll down my face, and my body would have this horrible internal trembling. My heart would be racing as if it were going to jump out of my chest.

Being in my bed instead of on the bathroom floor was a comfort. Tony would roll over, his arms would go around me, and his voice was gentle with his "Shhhh." I still kept thinking this had to be a nightmare.

In the morning, I awoke to the internal trembling. I didn't want to move, but I did—to the couch where I curled up in a ball. We went to church, and then we went by Mom and Dad's just to be together as a family.

We didn't say much, nor did we do anything, but we were together; it was the only way we could comfort one another. Once we got home, I got in my nightclothes. I really didn't want to talk to anyone. I curled up on the couch. I just wanted to sleep; that was the only reasonable escape right now.

The next day was the wake. It was going to be a very long day with a one-day service from two o'clock to eight o'clock. We all headed out for the one hour and forty-five minute ride. The tears rolled down my face most of the way. I listened to the tape of songs I had sung for Aunt Anita's funeral. I still couldn't believe this was happening, that Louie could actually be gone.

It felt as if I was in someone else's life. It wasn't possible that we were in hell again. We had spent the three days before Christmas at the Clinic waiting to see if Mom would make it through the second surgery in two months' time related to her heart. Less than nine months later, we are on our way to Louie's wake. If that's not hell, then I'm not sure what is.

We arrived early. The first hour was for family. As I walked up the steps of the funeral home, the tears came flooding down my face. *Oh, God, I can't do this. Please, can't we make some kind of a deal? Let's go back a few days. Please don't let this be a reality.* The funeral director came down the steps to help me. I was moving slowly. I wasn't in any hurry to get inside.

As I entered the room where Louie's body lay, I felt a rush of emotions; I wasn't sure how I would get through this. As I headed towards the casket, a loud sob escaped. It didn't seem like this could be my brother. Anita, Marie, and I stood at the casket in tears. I yelled at Louie and hit his body. Anita yelled at me, and I started apologizing and crying even more. I felt anger, sadness, and confusion. I had no idea how I would attempt to get through this day.

I went over to give kisses and hugs to Debi, the children, and the rest of the family. We all seemed to be in slow motion. Marie needed a hug and put her arms around me. Right now, it was all we could do to offer each other comfort. I don't remember much of the details. I think I have never seen so many flowers and plants. Louie was so well loved. Half of the flowers and plants had been kept in the garage; they wouldn't all fit in the funeral home. Joe, the funeral director, said that he stopped counting after eight hundred. We received between eight hundred and one thousand of our family and friends.

I went through the motions and did what I was expected to do. I remember listening to Linda, one of Louie's employees (who now feels like family), recounting Louie's last few minutes on earth. The night before, Louie had not been feeling well; he thought it was the flu. The next day he got up and told Debi he needed to pick up some papers at the Christmas store. Debi drove him, and he had the dry heaves during the whole twenty-five minute ride. Debi wanted to take him to the hospital, but he felt he had the flu. He made it up the steps to his office and asked Debi to get him some aspirin. He felt ill, and he began having pains in his chest and down his arm. Before Debi ran downstairs to get help, Linda said she buzzed him in his office to tell him Mom had called but said it wasn't important to call her later. She hadn't realized how ill Louie was. Linda especially mentioned this because she told Mom that those were the last words he heard, "Your mom called."

When Debi got back upstairs with help and called 9-1-1, Louie was on the floor with no heartbeat or respiration. The paramedics arrived and began working on him, then took him to the hospital where the code team worked for about an hour and a half. There wasn't anything that could be done. At least, now it made sense. He was in his store and not a video store, and he wasn't completely alone.

Some of the family members were going to stay with Debi and the children, but Tony and I decided it was best if we went home. Debi had the support she needed. I got into my nightclothes after showering and curled up on the couch. I just knew that if I slept long enough, eventually someone would have to wake me up and the nightmare would be over. When I awoke in the morning, for a split second I thought I had just had a terrible nightmare. But the internal shaking began, and the truth began to flood my thoughts: the terrible nightmare was actually a terrible reality.

We all got ready to go to the funeral. Each time I put some makeup on my face, the tears would wash it away. The realization that today is Louie's birthday is sinking in; he would have been forty-one years old. Instead of celebrating his birthday, we're going to his funeral. *Dear God, this truly is a nightmare. Please give me the strength to get through this.*

The drive to the funeral home seemed endless, yet to me we got there too quickly. I kept trying to fool myself into thinking that if time moved slowly, maybe, just maybe, someone would wake me up, and our lives could be as they were before. We arrived at the funeral home to pay our final respects and then to the church for the Mass. Although I can't remember the words, the priest gave a wonderful eulogy. He and Louie were friends, so his words were quite personal.

I remember Anita and me with our arms around each other, somehow trying to share the little strength we had between us. Anita's husband Sam and Tony were pallbearers. At the cemetery, my nieces gave a talk about their father that brought tears to everyone's eyes. We went to eat afterwards, and then Tony and Sam and the children went home. Anita and I stayed longer with Debi and the children, and then we spent time talking on the long ride home. Neither of us was sure how we are going to get through this. We both know our lives will be forever changed.

Much of those couple of days is a blur. Maybe this is a defense mechanism because to remember too much of it in detail would shatter my already broken heart even more. I'm not even sure how I will ever put my life together again.

3
Actual Journal Entries

∗ Somehow one expects the loss of a parent, hopefully at a ripe old age. One does not expect to lose a sibling, a brother, a dear beloved brother who was the heart of the family. One does not expect to bury a brother on his forty-first birthday. My heart is broken; words cannot express the pain. I have never experienced such unbearable pain. It almost drives you over the edge into a state of unconsciousness. It's heart-wrenching; it feels as if the heart has been torn out. There is no physical pain that could hurt worse because the human body could not endure it.

*Life will never be the same, for a piece of the puzzle is missing.

*As if the loss of my brother is not enough to bear, the anguish on my parents' faces, especially my mother's, is almost more than I can stand. There are no words to offer comfort; all I can do is hug, hold, kiss, and pray that somehow "love" can ease the hurt. How can she be comforted? A child she carried in her womb is no longer here. The pain and anguish is probably no less than what the Blessed Mother felt when she saw her son on the cross.

*I've heard time heals all wounds, but in this instance, time will ease our pain, but time will not heal, until we are reunited in heaven. How can it? A piece of the puzzle is forever gone. You can't put together what is no longer here.

The day after the funeral I called my friend Michelle and asked her if she could come over. She had said that if I needed anything to call. What I needed and I wanted was my brother back. Tony had to go back to work, and our son had an orthodontist appointment. I needed groceries but didn't want to take the chance of driving. When the boys went out in the yard to play, I sat on the couch and cried. I felt numb; I didn't want to do anything. *Dear God, this nightmare is still going on. When is someone going to wake me up?*

Michelle arrived and sat on the couch with me. I sobbed as she held me. I needed her strength now if there was any chance I was going to make it through this day. She dropped Tony and me off at the appointment, and she and Mike went to buy groceries. She picked us up, and when we got home, she and Mike had straightened the house, done the laundry, and had dinner cooking. She told me to rest. I lay down as the tears kept sliding down my cheeks. My eyes seemed to be like a leaky faucet. Drip, drip, drip. I couldn't seem to make it stop. I had no appetite, but I managed to eat a small amount of dinner.

Michelle cleaned up the kitchen and organized things before she went home. After she left, I went to bed, not knowing that Michelle would end up being one of my earthly guardian angels. It amazed me that life continued on with all the normal things of this earth. I wanted to stop the earth from rotating so that I could catch my breath. It also amazed me that I made it through another day without my Louie.

*Our family is very close. The closeness we feel now is unlike any imaginable. If you've had a falling out with a family member or friend, don't wait for tragedy to express your feelings. It may be too late. Even if you have never had a falling out, tell your family and friends that you care for them, even if you think they know how you feel.

My brother knew I loved him; we would tell each other every so often, but now it seems not often enough. If it's too difficult for you to say the words, write them, and if you can't write them, then find a card with someone else's words expressing your feelings. Don't wait another moment because life is but a moment in time. None of us knows how many moments we have left. Never in a million years would I have expected life to change so devastatingly, but it can, and it does in an instant. Don't wait. Tell someone how you feel. Keep close to those you love and close to God, for without him everything else is meaningless. There are no words of comfort, but faith in the Lord and one another will bring families through this journey together.

*It is one week since the Lord called Louie home. The heart remains broken. When I say the heart is broken, I mean it, in the literal sense; it actually hurts. It's not the type of pain, at least I think it's not, one experiences with a heart attack; it doesn't run through your chest, into your back, or down your arm. It stays in the area of your heart. You hope sleep will consume you so that the pain will stop. If you're lucky enough to go to sleep, when you awaken, you question for a brief second if the past week could have been a nightmare. Then the whole body shakes inside, the pain in your heart is still there, no trembling shows on the outside, and you realize it wasn't a cruel nightmare; it was a cruel reality. You drag yourself out of bed, to the couch, to the chair, maybe even outside, and you think, and you sob, and you ask why. *Dear Lord, why?*

*You feel anger, but you aren't sure who or what to feel angry at. You wait for the phone to ring because you want to hear some-one cares, someone understands if he or she has been through this. You don't want to answer the phone, because you don't want to have to tell the nightmare yet again, but you do. You go to the mailbox, to see who cares, who sent the cards, but you don't want to read the words and bring the heart-wrenching truth right up into your face again, but you do. Does it bring comfort? Yes, for an instant, and then the tears stream down the face, and the heart pains a little stronger.

*A neighbor stopped over, we talked briefly, and I told her my brother passed on. As she hugged me, and we cried, I remem-bered that she had lost a brother too. I asked her if the pain ever goes away. She said no, but that it eases with time. She told me to continue telling people all about my brother. "If the tears come," she said, "let them. After saying it about a million times, one day you'll realize that you'll actually say it without tears." I asked her if she felt she wanted to die after her brother died, she said no initially, but then she said maybe she did, but she has a family to take care of. I know I have a family also, but I'm not beyond the point of feeling as if I want to die.

The week has been filled with cards, calls, plants, and meals from friends. It's nice to know people care and want to help. Michelle and Colleen were with me every step of the way. If they weren't always able to be there physically, their thoughts, prayers, and phone calls were.

*You look at the reflection of yourself in the mirror. It looks like you, but something has changed. The hair may be disheveled, but bringing a brush through it can change it. The eyebrows may be furrowed; you can change that with a movement in the forehead.

The nose may be wrinkled, but that, too, you can change. The lips may be in a frown of sadness, but you can fake a smile. You realize it's the eyes; something is missing in the eyes. The color is the same, and redness in the whites from the tears that always remain on the brim of the lashes can be hidden with drops. Then you realize it's that sparkle, the sparkle put there with the love of your brother, from the teasing, joking, laughing, and love we shared. That sparkle can never shine again.

*You awake in the morning, and for a split second, you try to determine if it was all a nightmare; then the reality moves in. You survived another day and wake to a new morning. *Survive* is the appropriate word, because you can't call it living. Living is what you did before. Now it's surviving. Some moments you may feel guilty because you're still here and your loved one isn't. I feel as if a part of me is with Louie. I feel as if I could curl up in a ball and die. But how can I do that? I have a husband and two boys I love and adore. How do I heal myself? They deserve more than what I'm able to give right now. Will I ever be able to live again? I love them, and I want to be there for them the way I was before all of this—but how? How do I do that? Some days I feel as if I'm in the dark, and I can't find the light switch. Other days I find it, but it will only give me a little bit of light. How can I learn to take control of that switch and turn my light back on? There has to be a way. I just haven't figured out how to do it yet.

4
Michael's Story

﹡T he Lord brings comfort to us in a great many different ways. Sometimes even through our children. The weekend at work, my first after Louie's death, was so busy. We were short-staffed, and the acuity of several patients was high. On Sunday night I was driving home around 12:30 A.M. I don't remember thinking of anything specific. I was playing my tape of songs from Aunt Anita's funeral, and thoughts drifted from Louie to the hectic evening. After ten minutes or so, I noticed a beam projecting from the streetlights onto the windshield of my car from each light to the next. It continued the whole way home. When I got closer to home, the streetlights were fewer, so the beams projected from the moon. I've never noticed this before.

﹡Once I got home, I was tired, but I wasn't ready to sleep. I changed my clothes in the bedroom. Then I settled myself on the couch, turned on the fan with the wonderful humming sound to help me relax, and got the book I had been reading the last couple of days, *We Don't Die: George Anderson's Conversations with the Other Side*. I had read it two or three years earlier, but it was such a comfort and an excellent book that warranted reading again.

A few minutes went by. I heard three voices. Two were male, and I couldn't distinguish the third. I thought perhaps I had awakened Tony, and maybe he had turned on the radio, or maybe the neighbors were outside on this warm night. I checked on Tony, but he was snoring away, and as far as I could tell, no one was outside. I came back to the couch and started reading again.

*A little while later, Mike came out and said he couldn't sleep and wanted to lie out on the couch with me. I told him to sleep in my bed with Dad since he had to get up early for his first day of school. After Mike went to my room, I heard the voices again. It was as if when there is a party going on and you're standing a few feet away from a small group of people. You can hear their voices, but you are unable to interpret what they are saying. Only this time I said to myself, "That sounds like Louie," but I could not distinguish what he was saying. I wasn't sure what to think. I read a while longer, then turned off the lights, and finally fell asleep. I awoke sometime around 3:00 or 4:00 A.M. and looked into the dining room at my chandelier, and for a split second I thought I saw a figure. I blinked my eyes to clear my vision, and the figure was gone. I have no idea who or what it was. I thought, *First you're hearing things; now you're seeing things.* The next day I got the boys off to school and went back to bed. I was simply exhausted.

*The rest of the day I was in slow motion and never did get much accomplished. I talked to Mom twice. That evening, I remembered my experiences from the night before and told her about the lights, the voices, and the figure.

Mike had been sitting in the chair next to me. When he heard me tell Mom about hearing Louie's voice, Mike said, "Mom, I heard Uncle Louie's voice, too!"

Surprised, I said, "You did? What did he say?"

"I couldn't understand everything, but he said, 'I love you,' or 'I love you all and I'll keep you safe or ask God to keep you safe.' I'm not sure but something about safe." Mike went on to say that he was not sure if he was awake or dreaming, but he thinks he was awake because Daddy was snoring.

*Mom and I finished our conversation, and Mike and I talked. I explained to him, "You wouldn't want to make up stories about this, even if it was to make people feel better."

Mike said, "Mom, I would never do that." Then he asked if this was a good thing. I told him it was very good. He asked me to sleep with him that night. He said that he was a little bit frightened. I told him that this was nothing to be frightened of and that Uncle Louie would probably be his guardian angel now. He then shared he felt he knew why he heard his voice.

Michael said when he went to bed he was thinking about Uncle Louie and remembering all the teasing and all the names he called him, *Bichael*. (Mike called himself that when he was very young and couldn't pronounce his M's well). *Baerga* (Mike loved Carlos from the Indians club and so on). He said he remembered all the funny things he did and started to cry. He prayed to God and asked him if Uncle Louie could come and give him a hug, and then he fell asleep…I tried to figure out why I couldn't understand what Louie was saying…Maybe that night I only heard the voice because I wasn't meant to hear the words; it just may have been "Mike's hug."

*After this spiritual encounter, I did sleep with Mike that night, or I should say, tried to sleep. So I dozed. Mike was asleep in my arms. As I awakened, I looked around the room and into the hallway. As I focused my eyes, I saw the color orange swirling in the air and form the face of Christ and then disappear. I was hesitant to believe whether I really saw what I thought I saw; I've been so tired lately. I dozed again, and when I awoke, the same thing happened, except this time the image was closer and it lasted longer. Then I knew it was for real. I asked, *Okay, Lord. What are you trying to show or tell me?* It was such a comforting feeling. The third and final time, the orange swirled into the shape of the sun. Then it began to spin and disappeared. I settled into the bed with Mike curled next to me.

*The next day I gave some thought as to why I received this spiritual encounter. I think it's twofold—first, to let me know that Mike's experience and mine were real, and second, for comfort. The Lord works in mysterious ways, even through answering the prayers of our children.

5
Louie's Store

* I told Debi I would come as often as I could to help in the store—Louie's store—Louie's dream that came to life through his creative genius. Last year it was a magical store, Christmas World in Victorian Village. I still remember the excitement in my stomach as we walked through the door, and there he was, standing behind the counter in his Christmas World sweater with that smile on his face. Ironically, I went to the store three times that year instead of making my annual visit, taking different friends.

When visitors entered the store, the first sight they would see was forty to fifty Christmas trees for sale with bits of animation between the trees. To the immediate right was the counter with the cash register. Continue left past the counter, the first room to the right under the archway filled with hundreds and hundreds of Santas, brings you into the decorated tree room. In this room, visitors could find many ideas about how to decorate their own trees. There were trees decorated with teddy bears, instruments, Victorian style ornaments, even a forestland tree. Up above, the upside-down Christmas tree turned around and around.

The next room was the village room. Here enclosed in glass was Dickens' village, Department-56 Snow Village, and others—

more than one hundred different lighted ceramic houses and all the needed accessories to choose from. Louie displayed the houses in such a way that many people wanted to purchase the whole set of a certain style of houses and accents and have him set it up exactly the same as in the store.

The next room was the gift and collectible room. Customers could choose from inexpensive to expensive items, from simple to simply elegant.

Another room displayed the Old World Christmas Inge-Glass Ornaments enclosed in glass cases. Many pieces had a card telling the story about that particular ornament.

The nativity room was partly enclosed in glass with Seraphim angels and water globes. The back wall had two Christmas trees filled with angel ornaments. The opposite wall displayed Fontanini figures, nativities, and stables. Outside this room were several glass-enclosed cases with collectibles from Precious Moments, Snowbabies, Calico Kittens, and Cherished Teddies. Another room displayed thousands of different ornaments, as well as wreaths, wrapping paper, cards, bows, ribbons, and candles.

Once they are through browsing, shoppers can step through the doorway into the no-charge Winter Wonderland, an animated walk-through. I would get as much pleasure from seeing the display as I would from watching the faces of the store's visitors, especially the children's. Santa and his elves busy making toys... Prancer, the talking reindeer... Bubbles, the reindeer, blowing bubbles with the elves... and Santa making his list and checking it twice were just a few of the sights one would see before reaching the cobblestones and taking a step back into Christmas past with Victorian street vendors, Christmas carolers, and much more.

Next was my favorite part of the walk-through, and Louie's too, where you see and feel the true meaning of Christmas—the hand-painted, imported life-sized Fontanini Nativity set. I don't think there is another store in the state that has one indoors. Louie had dedicated the Nativity to our grandparents who died. The Nativity was definitely Louie's pride and joy. It was how Louie based his life, as a true Christian who always thought about others.

At the exit of the walkway was a donation box. Toward the end of the holiday season Louie would add a substantial amount of his own money and then make wishes come true for those who were less fortunate.

I think because we were less fortunate financially when we were children, Louie focused on anonymously making others' wishes come true. God knew what he did for others, and that was good enough for Louie.

As I headed out to the store, my mind went into different directions. I said a rosary to pass the time and keep my mind occupied.

I arrived before Debi. My head said, "You're doing the right thing." My heart said, *You're fooling yourself. He's not in there.* When Debi arrived and we entered the store, I had a rush of emotions, as a tear or two slid down my face. Maybe he wasn't there in the physical sense, but he was there in spirit.

It was difficult being there without him, but I'm hoping, as time goes on, it will also be a healing place.

6
One Month

∗ It's been a month. I still can't say that we are living; *functioning, surviving* are the more appropriate words. Spending time with Debi and the children and other family members also brings comfort. Each of us continues to mourn in our own way—but togetherness, the closeness, brings comfort. Being in Louie's store brings comfort; so much of him, of his dream, is there. It's a way to feel the closeness to him. I learned through Louie's example that if you work hard, dreams can come true. His did in his Christmas World and Victorian Village. It just hurts so much that he's not here to be a part of his dream.

*I've come to the realization that it's not important to be stronger, wiser, or better than anyone; it's only important that I become the best for myself in all things that I do. For if I'm the best I'm capable of being, no one, not even I, could or should expect more.

*I know that Tony is having a difficult time with how I'm not adjusting to Louie's death. Tony's way of dealing with grief is different from mine. I don't know how to make him understand how I feel. I only know that right now I can't feel any different. I don't know how to heal myself. I don't know how to let him know that I love him still. I'm just missing my brother so terribly. I didn't ask for this grief in my life. I don't want this grief in my life. I didn't want my life to be turned upside down and inside out. What will happen if I'm in a state of mourning for the rest of my life?

The realization that Louie has died is slowly trying to creep in. My head says quietly, *In order to get through this, you must let reality in.* My heart then screams, *Never, never will I let it in!* For my heart to let it in could destroy, shatter, tear apart my already wounded, broken heart. How much can I expect it to take? If it breaks completely in half, how will I ever, ever begin to repair it? For if you cut me, will I not bleed? If you slap me, will I not sting? If you say mean, hateful words to me, will I not cry? But if you hold me, try to understand me, will you try to understand what I'm feeling? If you kiss me, say kind things to me, will I not begin to heal? Will I not try to pick up the broken pieces of my life? I don't know...but I can try...

*My head tells me I want to go on, I need to go on, I have a husband, children, a brother, two sisters, other family and friends who need me, and I still have Louie, in my heart. I will forever carry him in my heart. But then my heart will tell me it's too hard. I don't have the energy to work through this. Things don't feel right ... my job... my life...nothing feels right. Life will never be the same. This grief hurts; it hurts like hell. I can't help that it feels like this. I tell my family we'll get through this together, one day at a time, but sometimes I'm not even sure myself if I'll get through this.

*I've recently realized that I never fully grieved for Aunt Anita. Each time a patient at work died, I'd set it aside, especially Ashley. Then Louie died, and that changed it all. It all came to a total accumulation of grief that overflowed like a pot boiling over on the stove. I've reached my limit, and somehow I have to begin the process of recovery. But I don't know how ...where do I start?

*Mom and I began a six-week bereavement support group. It helped. It was a place I could be myself, feel whatever I was feeling. I could cry, I could release the pain, and no one told me to stop or I shouldn't feel this way. I could be me...somehow there is comfort in being around people who are experiencing the same types of feelings you are.

*I tell myself that I'm going to get organized. I feel as if every aspect of my life is in disarray, and I hate it.

The pieces don't seem to fit anymore, and I feel as if I have forgotten how to make it work anymore. People tell me that I have to go on, that's what my brother would want, but no one tells me how. Do people think that the ways we feel and act are premeditated? In some ways, I don't seem to have a choice. Do I? To grieve and mourn or shove it under the carpet? It hurts like hell, and I can't make it stop. Everything is falling apart around me. I'm so sensitive about everything. I'm not even sure how to interpret others' comments. I don't want to feel this lousy. I feel as if I've lost control, and I hate that the most.

*When you lose someone so important in your life, your head tells you, *Stay busy, keep your mind occupied, and I'll let you forget the pain just for today.* You think, *Great, I'll do that.* It's working. It has been a whole hour or two, except your head seems to forget that your heart has a stake in this. Because this loss, any loss to you, is a matter of the heart, and the heart always wins. Smack. You'll see, smell, hear, think, whatever, something that reminds you of that person, and as if someone slapped you in the face, the pain is there again. Actually, it never left; it just dulls sometimes like that dimmer on the light switch, except with a dimmer switch you can control how soft or bright you want the light to be. You can't control the intensity of the pain you feel.

*Now along with the pain usually come the tears, and at times, the tears can be a bit easier to control. Sometimes you can choke them back for a while. I have found if I let them flow, I can generally pick myself up and carry on with my daily living. On other occasions, I cry and cry and cry...If I am in a place where I don't want to let the floodgates open, usually distracting myself by my surroundings or if possible by a funny memory of Louie generally stops the tears from flowing until I can get to a place to let them open. But certainly, it is best to let the tears flow when you feel you need to. It gives you more relief.

7
Two/Three Months

✱We're heading into two months, and the fact that I have not awakened from this nightmare is making me think that I'm not going to wake up, that somehow I'm going to have to learn to live this way. At times, even the music around me can be annoying. I am now beginning to realize that I cannot expect others to feel the way I do. Just because my life is drastically different doesn't mean everyone else's is. While I may feel this pain of grief—as an ever-present toothache, throbbing at times, lingering at others—that such a wonderful person is no longer with us, I personally feel that everyone should feel the loss. But I know that is not a reality. People go on with their lives just as they did before because it's my loss, not theirs.

*I think in the back of my mind that I thought after two months I would feel different, but I don't know exactly in what way. The grief and pain are still here. The intensity is not always as the sharp, stabbing constant pain it was two months ago, but it's still there. My head and heart continue to battle. And my heart still *always* wins! My heart is broken, and it still hurts. The intensity has decreased, but the pain isn't gone.

Mom asked one day while how we were going to get through the holidays. I told her, "I don't know. I haven't been too good at survival lately." That wasn't fair. What I should have said is

"I'm not sure. I guess we'll figure it out when we get to them."
My heart isn't ready to deal with all those emotions. Sometimes I
feel as if I'll explode. I cry. Sometimes I can't hold it back. My
head keeps telling me that Louie is not here any more, and my
heart shouts, *Don't say that!*

*As Mom and I wrapped up the six weeks with the bereave-
ment support group, it helped. Much of the time it provided a
temporary relief, but it was a relief. I must admit I went to the
group for Mom's sake, as difficult as it was. I didn't want her to
go alone. Listening to how torn up she is over the loss of her
Louie was hard, and so was knowing that there isn't a thing I can
do to make her feel any better. On the other hand, even though I
didn't expect to, I received the group's benefits. I learned that
what I am feeling is very normal. My feelings of wanting to be
with my brother are normal, but acting upon them or dwelling on
those thoughts is abnormal, and if one continues to feel this way,
further help may be needed to overcome these feelings. Alice, the
group's facilitator, is a remarkable woman. As she walks into the
room, her compassion shows. There is no magic recipe to get
through the grief process more quickly. She shared that grieving
and mourning are a lot of hard work, and there is no quick fix-it.
The grief process and the time it takes to work through it is different for everyone.

*We're approaching the three-month point, and time contin-
ues to move on. The pain hasn't moved on. The intensity isn't as
sharp, but the pain is still there. The shock begins to wear off, and
reality tries to sneak in. My heart and head continue to battle. My
heart still says, *No, he couldn't have died.* My head says, *Yes, it
is a reality.* The feeling of not being in control remains. I attempt
to gain some control by covering up the pain. You can fix your

hair, put on some makeup, put on a smile, yet the whole time your insides feel as if your stomach is pushed up in your chest, and the rest of your insides are up in your throat.

*I think it still hasn't sunk in—the reality that I may live thirty, forty, fifty years without my Louie, without hugging, kissing, or touching that handsome face again. He can't really be gone. This has to be a cruel joke, a nightmare. I'm living in this nightmare, and I can't wake up. I've gone from having a difficult time sleeping to all I want to do is sleep. I can't get enough sleep— I'm always tired—but while I'm sleeping, I don't have to think or feel the pain.

*Halloween recently passed, and I realized I had been wearing a mask. I can't pinpoint when I started to wear it, but when you're around people, you wear the mask. Eventually, you get so used to wearing the mask that you forget you have it on. Sometimes you get frightened and think if you take the mask off, you may not be able to put it back on again. I have found that the "everything is okay" mask is extremely tiring. But I'm afraid if I take it off, I'll have to accept the fact that Louie is actually not with us on earth any longer. I'm just not ready to accept this. I'm scared. How are we supposed to get through this? The holidays are right around the corner. I've been trying to prepare; I have to for the children. But I could curl up in a corner and sleep through the holidays. I don't feel festive. I need to focus on the fact that in our religion Christmas is a celebration of the birth of our Lord, not on the thought that Louie won't be here, except I haven't figured out how to do that. I don't know how to heal myself. As the fourth month fast approaches, the intensity of the pain and the sting continue to ease ever so slightly but hasn't left. The heart is broken—and still aches.

8
Four Months

* It's been four months. I'm not feeling any different. I still miss Louie an awful lot, still don't understand why this happened. I don't know if I ever will. In the midst of this holiday season, it's hard to celebrate when someone very special is not here anymore, and you remember that it was your special person. It feels as if you're standing in the ocean...the waves are calm as they come in and around your feet ...you feel the warm sand between your toes as the warmth of the sun caresses your face. All of a sudden the waves are bobbing at your knees, then a gigantic wave you didn't expect comes out of nowhere...it's a little more than you think you can handle to balance yourself...it almost knocks you off your feet, sets you off guard again. That's how grief feels sometimes, and your heart still aches.

*Sometimes you try to figure out why this happened, and you think the grief will be better next week or month. Then you get to next week or month, and grief isn't really any better. I wonder if I'm ever going to feel some type of normalcy again. I realize I have no control. No matter what I do, how many tears I shed, how much pain I feel, or how much I pray, he's not coming back. It hurts so very much. I do the best I can even if it doesn't feel good enough. I pray that he is aware to how much he is loved and is missed. I pray to our Lord to give me strength to get through another day.

*What seems interesting to me is I haven't found much written that tells how to get through this—the grief, the mourning, and the feelings. What's normal? What should one expect? From working my way through this, I have learned there is no one set way. The losses are different; people grieve differently, so we do the best that we can. We stumble through and hope that whatever steps we take to get through the grief process help us to come out feeling a little bit better with each phase we work through.

*Everyone's grief and mourning will be different. At times I think I'm doing so well, I'm managing, I'm getting through this, yet I know I'm not at an acceptance point. Then it hits hard, like the feeling that you're standing in the ocean. The grief is there, the pain is there, and you think I guess I'm not doing as well as I thought I was. You try really hard to pull yourself together. I'm blessed with a husband and children and family. I try to pull myself together for them. It is very scary, knowing it may be many years before I am reunited with my brother. Sometimes it is hard to imagine living that long without him.

*There is no choice; we have no control. All the tears in the world and the feelings and emotions of every single person can't change this. If all people in the world would pause for ten seconds and say they understand and they wish that this hadn't happened to our family—that won't change anything. All the prayer in the world right now can't reverse this situation. I think my mind knows that Louie is in a better place. I try to find happiness somewhere in my heart for him. He doesn't have to endure pain, grief, and heartache anymore. My heart keeps battling with me. Somewhere in the back of my mind I keep thinking that this is the longest nightmare I've ever had and soon somebody's got to be merciful and wake me. I know that's not going to happen. Even as I say these words, I still can't believe he's gone from this earth. Each time I enter his store, I expect him to be standing behind the counter, coming up to me, giving me a kiss with that special smile on his face. Day by day, I think that if I get through today, tomorrow will be better. Sometimes it is; sometimes it isn't. In some ways it can be worse because the shock is wearing off, and reality is trying to set in. I don't know how we're going to get through these holidays. I just don't know.

*It still seems incomprehensible to me that Louie can be gone. I look on my refrigerator and see his picture, and he seems bigger than life to me. I don't know how I'm ever going to get to a point of acceptance. It still seems so unfair. At times I still feel angry, I still feel cheated, and I don't know when it's ever going to feel different. I don't know when I'm going to feel human again, as if the pieces are put together instead of so dismantled. I know that the discomfort I still have in my chest is because my heart is broken. I don't know how to heal that heart. I don't know how to mend it. I don't know how to put it back together again. It still feels like a nightmare to me. It's a little over four months already. Why? I just want to know why? I want to know he's okay. I want to know that we're going to be okay too. I want to know that we're all going to get through this. I want to know that we'll be able to function and that, although we're never going to be normal again, we will get to some point of normalcy.

*I still want to be angry, but I don't know who to be angry with. I want to cry. I want to be me again. I don't know how to do that. I don't know how to be the person I was before all this happened. I want to hold Louie again. I want to talk to him and have him talk back to me. I want to kiss him again, I want to hug him again, and I want to see him standing behind that counter in his store again. To me, thirty-six years was not long enough to have my brother. I want more! I want to feel alive again; I don't know how to do that. He was the one who could make us laugh, bring us to tears from the laughter, and make us feel as if we would wet ourselves from laughing so hard. Why do his children have to grow up without a father, his wife without her husband? Does the pain ever stop, ever go away?

*Life continues. The pain continues. The heart and head continue to battle. I feel as if I'm stuck in the same spot of mourning. In the movie *Groundhog Day*, Bill Murray's character kept reliving the same day over and over until he got it right. Sometimes that is how mourning can feel…the same grieving…the same pain in my heart…the same tears. I guess I haven't got it right yet; I haven't gotten beyond the spot I'm stuck in. Sometimes the feeling is like nothing, deep emptiness, and at other times, I feel as if I'm fighting to keep my head above the water, to keep from drowning in my own tears.

*Sometimes I think there's a very fine line between sane and insane, and if I let go, I may end up on the insanity side. The mind just doesn't want to accept the fact that Louie is actually gone. I'm not sure how to get the brain to accept this as a reality. Which do I try to convince first—the brain or the heart? How do I get my heart and brain to accept this loss at the same time so that they can each bear part of the truth and give me half a chance of keeping my brain from crossing over to insanity and my heart from breaking completely in half? Will I ever find any of these answers?

*When I think in retrospect of this tragedy that happened, it seems as if I would be better off to feel the way I felt when I received the phone call of Louie's passing. The numbness… it was almost a non-feeling. It was such a state of shock and disbelief… the whole body was numb, except for the internal shaking and the pain in the heart. I don't know… maybe that's even better than this void, this pain and sorrow… emptiness… it's just so very difficult. I keep thinking grief has to feel better or be easier, and it doesn't really get any easier or feel any better. The intensity continues to ease, but everything else is still there.

9
Earthly Angels

Michelle continues to be my guardian angel. Our relationship has grown. I'll never be able to show my gratitude for all she has done, just listening to me on some days and on others keeping me busy shopping and such so I don't have time to think. Michelle and Gil came over for dinner and helped put up my Department-56 Snow Village. It was difficult to decide if I wanted to display it this year. The Snow Village (ceramic houses and complementary pieces) was something Louie and I had started together last year. He helped me pick out the pieces.

When I saw Louie for the last time at the wedding, he told me about the new piece to the Snow Village, Santa's castle. Before I had an opportunity to see the piece, I told Debi to save one for me. I knew that if he liked it that much, it had to be special. As we took the piece out of the box, the tears rolled down my face. All I could think about was the look on his face as he talked about the new pieces that had arrived at his store. The castle is my favorite piece. It's my last connection with my brother. I will always treasure it.

As I wrapped up my last day helping at Louie's store, again I felt a rush of emotions. As Debi and Linda and I hugged and said our good-byes, the tears rolled down our faces. I was driving home thinking about the couple of spiritual encounters we had. At times when we were talking about Louie and tears were streaming down our faces, the lights would flicker on and off in the store. We knew no one could be teasing us because we were the only three in the store. When Anita and I were putting lights on the trees and talking about Louie, one of us said, "Louie would like it that way," and the lights on the tree flickered several times. As I left the store, I had a feeling of contentment. I went in all those weekends not only to help Debi but also to get some form of closure in regard to his store because so much of the store was a part of him. I'm hoping, as time goes on, this will help me put that part of Louie, his dream, into proper perspective.

Initially, I felt Debi should keep the store open, so his dream can live on. After being in the store and helping, I see how much work it takes, and I feel she should do what is best for her and the children. My support is with her. The animation was not up this year because it was his creative genius that brought the magic to the store. What surprised and at times was hurtful to me was the insensitivity of some of the visitors to the store. They would come to the counter and ask, "How do you get into the walkway?" When we would tell them it wasn't put up this year, some would turn and walk out. Some would visit the rest of the store and either make a purchase or not. Others would ask why. I would tell them it was because my brother had done all the work of the walkway and that he had died in August. The responses were varied. Some said, "Gee, that's too bad. Are you gonna do it next year?" One woman stood at the door, stamped her foot, and said, " I drove all the way out here and wasted all that gas for nothing." A handful of people took the time to tell us how truly sorry they were. They shared how much joy the animated walkway had brought them over the years; they had made a visit to the store part of their holiday tradition. They said how beautiful the displays were and that the animation would be greatly missed. It was nice to know others shared our belief and had enjoyed Louie's dream as much as we did. Gratefully, I had taken videos of the walkway a couple of times, so whenever I want my mind refreshed, I'll put the videos on and let the tears flow.

Colleen and I continue to get together as often as we can. We talk on the phone just about every day. I feel bad that her grandmother is not doing well, so she's out at her mom's all the time. I'm having such a difficult time that I don't even feel as if I've given her any support after all she has done for me. Maybe trying to heal myself for others would be a start toward trying to mend my broken heart.

10
The Holidays

* As Christmas draws ever closer, the grieving intensifies. It hardly feels as if it is a holiday. I went through the motions—the tree, the presents, candy making, the cookie making — with Michelle's help and for the sake of the children. As for me, I'm not sure what I feel. I can't feel festive. I try to put on a happy face for the children. It would be impossible to explain to them how I feel. Sometimes this mourning seems as if it has been going on forever, and I wonder if I'll ever feel a heart of joy again.

*It's Christmas Eve morning. The emptiness remains. I'm trying to busy myself with the holiday tasks—preparing the homemade cookie and candy trays, gathering the gifts for Mom's house—while my mind continues to wander to spiritual things, to Louie. Is he happy? Does he know how very much we miss him? Is he with us, trying to comfort us, only we're not aware of his presence? They must celebrate in heaven. What's the celebration like? Or is he so wrapped up with heaven's preparations that he's not even aware of ours? How can we get through this season without him? So many questions…I have so very many questions, but I'm not receiving any answers.

*I believe in my heart he is in the better place. Why can't I get my head to believe it? I have faith, I have a strong faith in God, so why am I faltering? God plucked or allowed Louie to be plucked from us just as a gardener has the right to pluck his precious rose that he spent so much of his time nurturing. But those of us who are left in this garden of life need some knowledge, some understanding, some form of communication with our Louie. Why must it always be on faith alone? We are servants of the Lord...I can't imagine that he wants to see us suffer when a nod of his head, a dream, a voice, a vision could ease our pain immensely. God allowed me answers with Grandma through dreams five months after she left this world. Aunt Anita appeared to me in a dream two days after she died. With Louie, it is almost five months and nothing, at least nothing that I'm aware of. My heart aches for him...I miss him so much ...nothing I do can heal myself. I don't know where to go for the answers. God and Mom are usually where I seek some answers...right now Mom doesn't have any herself, and I don't know...God's line seems to be busy.

Christmas was a bittersweet day. We all went to Mom and Dad's for dinner. It was comforting to be with one another, but there was an obvious void. Mom served a different meal than we traditionally have. Debi brought a candle that we lit and placed on the table in Louie's memory. Mom hung a stocking with his name on the fireplace. We didn't play our traditional game with cards and swapping the presents. Louie was the one who made it fun. He would try to hide presents so that no one would steal them, always taking the biggest boxes. Last year, I had wrapped a goofy headband with springs and glitter balls on the end. I had told everyone to make sure Louie ended up with that box. Of course, he did, and he wore that stupid headband the rest of the game. We laughed so hard. We never knew what he'd do next.

Mom did well for the sake of the grandchildren. She planned a carnival with them without our knowing. We went down into the basement to the carnival, and this brought us to tears. When Louie was a child, he always had summer carnivals in the back yard. Children would come from several streets away to be at Louie's carnival.

When the time to exchange presents came, I knew this would be tough. Each year the children would perform a play. They would practice after dinner, and we would go down to the basement to watch. Last year Mom and the children performed a play about "Old Bufona," an Italian Christmas story. Mom played Old Bufona. Unbeknown to Mom, Louie had found an Old Bufona figure to give to her at Christmas. Debi gave it to her from him and a male angel from her and the children. The river of tears flowed. I know Mom will treasure it always; it is on her fireplace mantel, her last present from her son.

I think Christ received the best birthday gift of all, our Louie.

11
Changes

*Mom and Dad left for Arizona two days after Christmas for a needed change. I'm hoping the change of climate and seeing all of Mom's relatives will bring them some comfort. I'm for just about anything that will bring Mom comfort. I'll miss them, but I think this is what they need right now.

*The New Year has arrived, and I admit I'm frightened, anxious, and relieved all at the same time. I'm frightened of what the year will bring. I'm not sure if physically and emotionally I could handle any more tragedy. In many respects, I'm anxious and relieved to make an attempt at accepting what has happened and to try to start anew. Time has not mended my broken heart. They say that time heals all wounds, but I don't think I'll be completely healed for the rest of my life. I think that all you learn with time is control. You can try to control the tears, but the pain remains ever an ache—sometimes sharp, sometimes dull, but always there.

*I have found that when you go through a tragedy like this, you keep trying to make changes in your life. Depending on the relationship you shared with that person, the death can be such a devastating change. I want life to be the way it was, and that's not possible. So I continue to make changes, but it can be a repetitious cycle. No matter how many changes you make, there is not a thing you can do to get life the way it was before; that's the most

most frustrating thing of all. The tragedy can change your essence, your soul, so much, that you almost feel as if you're a different person. Louie's death was something I had no control over. The truth is there are many things in life we cannot control; whether we like it or not, we have a choice to make—to live with the fact that our loved one has died or fight that fact for the rest of our lives.

*When I would attend a funeral, like most people, I never really knew what to say. I said things like, "I'm sorry about the death of…or I'm sorry for the loss of…". That is one of the changes I have made. There are no words that can really make anyone feel better. At least I haven't found any. So now I say something such as, "I know there are no words to ease your pain, I'll pray for you. If I can do anything for you, I'm only a phone call away." I find it difficult to tell someone that I know what they are going through or that I know how they feel, because there are so many variables with relationships. Can someone really know how another person truly feels about their loss? Except that it hurts like hell.

*I doubt that anyone likes to go to funerals, but it does make a difference to attend if possible. Initially, I couldn't remember if someone was at the funeral home, because of the number of people we received that day. Attending the wake or funeral does show people you are concerned, and for me the presence of friends at the funeral home meant more than any card, any flowers, or any words one could have spoken. But the calls, cards, and flowers were sincerely appreciated from the ones who couldn't be there.

*When I woke up this morning, I cried and felt an overwhelming sadness. It didn't dawn on me until later in the day when Anita mentioned that of course, I'd be feeling sad; we buried Louie six months ago today. I hadn't given it any thought earlier. How did I let it slip my mind? I still miss him so deeply. It is such an over-whelming loss. In many respects I feel as if I've been carrying a monkey on my back, or a monster has been chasing me. I'm very, very exhausted from trying to wear the mask every day. I need to try to get some peace. I need to try to take steps towards healing, and I don't really know how to do that. My heart and head still battle.

*Sometimes I feel as if I'm crying inside. No one knows it, for I've gotten good at keeping my true feelings hidden. Mike and I talked on the way home from Michelle's. I'm so flabbergasted at how intuitive he is at eleven. He knew I was sad; it was hard to wear the mask today. I told him I was missing Uncle Louie. He asked how going to a support group would help when all the people there were sad too. As we talked, he told me he still misses Uncle Louie. He asked if support groups were for children. I said that tonight's was not, but there are groups that are only for children. He said he didn't really feel he needed one, that hearing Uncle Louie's voice had made him feel so much better. The innocence of children sometimes amazes me.

*It is six months already. I feel in my heart that Louie is in heaven. It bothers me that when I've dreamed of him a few times since his death; he looks so solemn, and I can never remember what he tells me in the dream. I don't know how to resolve this, to gain peace with this. The support group helped, but again, it was temporary help. When I spoke with Alice today, the group's fa-cilitator, I told her I thought I had a functional depression. I can do my daily chores—cook, do laundry, take care of the children—but when it comes to any extras, I don't have the energy for it. I'm quite content lying on the couch and going to sleep. Somehow, I don't think that's how the rest of my life should be spent, but I just haven't figured out how to get beyond this right now...how to live again...instead of function...instead of survive.

*Michelle offered to go to the support group with me. I've spent a lot of time with her, and our friendship has continued to grow. There are days when I don't know what I'd do without her. It's comforting being with someone who cares. What she tells me is true. I don't have control over this, and nothing I do can change it. I have to find a way of accepting it...I don't know if I can ever accept it...maybe I can learn to accept it even though I'll never get over it ...I need to find a way to go on with life...I don't know how to come out of the pain I'm feeling...how to make this pain go away....I don't know how to make this heart stop hurting.

*I still feel guilt because it's not fair to my husband and children to keep feeling the way I do. A part of me feels this isn't right. Maybe if the Lord could just let Louie come to me in a dream or a vision or some type of answer, something so I know that he's happy. The fact that he appears solemn in my dreams bothers me so much. If part of his solemn appearance is because we are having such a difficult time dealing with his death, then somehow, somebody has to let us know. I don't want him to be solemn where he is. Heaven is too beautiful a place from what I can imagine, and I know I can't imagine it fully.

* I know he has received his eternal reward, and I would feel awful if he couldn't fully enjoy it because of me—because I'm having a hard time letting go. I never got to say goodbye. I never got to let him know how much I truly love him and how much he means to me...how very proud I was of him...the things he did in the store...how he patterned his life for his children to see...how important family was to him...his relationship with Mom...how he would bring happiness to others with his displays and anima-

tion in his store…giving of himself…if there was a way to have even one more moment with him, until we can be together in eternity. He was the one who always helped us get through this kind of thing. I just need someone to tell me how to get through this…to show me the way so that I can be at peace…so that he can be at peace…so that we all can be at peace until we meet again in heaven.

12
A Letter from Louie

*I came home exhausted from a twelve-hour shift, and I have to go back for another tomorrow. I awoke at 4:00 A.M. I couldn't sleep. So much was going through my head. I moved to the couch so that I wouldn't disturb Tony. After tossing and turning and my brain being on overload, I decided to sit at the kitchen table to write. I turned on a soft light, got something to drink, and started putting on paper what had been going through my mind. The following is what I put on paper that early February morning.

A Letter from Louie
I know how bad you're hurting, and I know how much you miss me.

I haven't really left you. I'm here because I know you need me.

I know you want to hold me tight, and even though you may not know, I often hold you in my arms to try to comfort you. If I see this isn't helping you, it makes me solemn too.

I realize the pain you're feeling, but you must try to let that go, for I'm all right in heaven. I'm really not alone.

The loved ones that went before me are here to hold me tight. I share with them, for they know the love we shared on earth.

My love for you hasn't changed. You must remember this. I

love you more than you could ever guess, for the love we feel in heaven is so overwhelming at times that it almost hurts. Heaven is so beautiful. There are no words to describe the beauty and surroundings that have become my life. This doesn't mean I have forgotten you, for that will never be, for life is now more peaceful, joyous, and much more free. If you could only get a glimpse of how happy I will be, as soon as I know you're all right and set my spirit free.

I know you may not realize that you're tying me to tears. I want to help you dry your tears and replace them with a smile.

I want you to start thinking of the joy we shared, the laughs we had, and the memories we made together.

I know this isn't easy, but you really must go on. Your work on earth isn't finished there, and life will go on.

It's a choice that you have to make—to let the days roll by or to live each day in your warm and loving way.

Keep my memory tucked inside, always in your reach, but don't keep me right in front, so no one else can see you.

Remember that your time on earth really isn't through. It may be many years for you, but to me, it's a twinkling of God's eye. That's okay. You are strong, and when your work is done and God calls you to our home, I will be there with open arms to kiss you and hold you tight, along with all our other relatives to bring you to the light. There are no tears in heaven, so begin to dry your eyes.

Remember that I love you, and know that I am with you, just in a different way. So go on now, be strong for us and for the others on the earth. One day when we reunite, we'll never have to part, but for now you must let me go and carry me in your heart.

Your Louie

*The above experience is difficult to put into words, but I'll try. When the writing was completed, I went to the top of the paper and wrote A Letter from Louie. I didn't actually hear my Louie's voice; I wasn't always aware of what was being put on the paper. At times I cried. When the experience was over, I put everything away to get ready for work. When I shared the letter with Colleen a couple of days later, I began to cry. I hadn't realized what some parts said. She felt that the letter was from Louie. I called Mom in Arizona and shared it with her. I told her that I wondered if this truly could be from Louie, since nothing like this had ever happened to me before. She suggested I ask for confirmation that it was from Louie. So that night when I went to bed, I said in my head, *Louie, was that truly from you?* I dreamed of Louie that night. He entered a room with his arms open and a smile on his face. I went into his arms crying and told him how much I missed him. I can't remember if he said anything to me. That was the first time since his death he had a smile on his face in one of my dreams. I believe what I wrote was truly a letter from my Louie.

13
Getting Stronger

Today marked the nine-month point since Louie went home to Jesus. Things have changed over the nine months. Relationships have changed. Our family has changed drastically. Louie's dying has changed many aspects of all of our lives. Mom does have her occasional good days, but most of her days seem wrapped in the deep mourning of Louie. I mourn Louie, I grieve Louie just as I know my other siblings do, and in some respects I feel that I'm mourning the loss of my mother. It is difficult on a day-to-day basis. Even though I know Louie is in heaven, I believe the letter that I received was from him, but even with the confirmations, the experiences, my other siblings have had, we still feel the emptiness.

*At this nine-month point, actually since the letter at the six-to-nine-month period, I've spent time trying to write how I felt when the phone call came at work telling me that Louie died. I have come to the realization that no matter how many years it is before God calls me home and I'm reunited with Louie, I'm never going to accept the fact that he is not here anymore. I feel that's okay, if I don't accept it. There are a lot of things in this world we can't accept, but in order to change my life, from surviving, to functioning and getting back to living, which is what I truly feel in my heart Louie would want, I have to move on. I have to get myself to a point from just letting the days roll by to living again.

*This is *not* an easy thing to do. Some may be able to do it in a few months, depending on how they feel about death, their relationship with the person, and whether the death was expected, and so on. These things play a part in when you come to terms or how quickly you can get through the grief process. It's different for everyone. No one can say I should have been over this three months ago, or I shouldn't be over it for another two years. I don't think death of this magnitude is going to be easily accepted. I don't think death of a loved one is always accepted. But I have found I have to learn to live with it. I think that is the bottom line; that is what I've been feeling. I am still one of five siblings, I have three siblings on earth and one I carry in my heart. The fact is that unless things drastically change with our mother, we've not only lost a brother but also lost a mother.

*I don't see any joy in her eyes anymore. I don't hear laughter in her voice. I'm not saying she should be over this, because she's never going to get over this, like the rest of us. If I can't accept this, how would I expect my mother to? I can't; I don't. She has had and still has tremendous health problems, and she says things like, "I want to get in bed and curl up and sleep until it is my time to go." "If I start having chest pains again, I'm not going to tell anyone; I'm just going to let it happen." She's not watching her diet, her cholesterol is high, and she is not exercising. This makes Louie's dying so much more difficult because I don't feel my mother's time is up yet, but she's going to push herself prematurely to death.

She has grandchildren and children who love her. A couple of days ago, when I walked into her house, she was crying. Her eyes were puffy; tears were rolling; her movements in the kitchen were slow, as usual, the way one moves when in severe pain.

Temporarily something snapped in me, seeing her in this kind of shape over and over again. I did something I had never done to my mother before. I grabbed her by the shoulders, not hard, and looked her straight in the eye. As tears were rolling down my face, I said, "Mom, you've got to stop this. You're making yourself sick. You've got to get hold of yourself."

She started crying harder and saying, "Don't yell at me!"

I said, "Maybe that's what you need right now."

*The death of a sibling, the death of anyone, changes so many aspects of our lives. It's difficult to explain all the true feelings with this. We're trying to get our lives back in order. Sometimes being around Mom has a way of bringing us down again. I was hoping that being around us and seeing that we're trying to get through this would help bring her spirits up a little. I'm not naïve enough to think that any one of us would be able to replace Louie. None of us would want to or even try to; Louie is a hard act to follow. I know one child cannot replace the other to a parent. We would always tease Mom on the holidays about rolling out the red carpet, Louie's here. She would come out of the room and practically run into the kitchen, barreling through whomever was in her path to get to Louie. We would laugh and enjoy watching the love burst between them.

*The fact that none of us can put a smile on her face anymore frightens me. I know the feelings of being able to move on. Whether you accept the death of a loved one or choose to put your life together again has to come from within as you start to heal. I've experienced this. I still doubt I will ever be fully healed. My heart will always remain broken because of his death.

Why, Lord, why, out of all of us siblings, why did you take Louie? In many respects Louie was Mom's lifeline. We all knew that about their relationship. I think there were a lot of reasons that he was. We all accepted this. There was no jealousy or animosity. It was that Italian mother-eldest son thing. I asked the Lord, "Why didn't you take me?"

*What truly frightens me with my mother is there are only two or three things that will help her come to out of this. First, if the Lord would allow her to have a vision of Louie or come to her in a dream. She would know it's him and no one else, and he would tell her to go on, because it's not her time yet. Second, and I don't think this is going to happen—my mother would come to terms with Louie's death and find a way to go on with her life—to have moments of joy with the children and grandchildren here on earth. We love her so deeply. Third, and this frightens me the most, that she will fail to take care of herself by not eating the right foods or exercising, and she will have a heart attack or worse.

Many people say getting through the first year is the hardest; then it gets easier. I'm hoping that's true for Mom, that she is going to try, whether it's two, five, or twenty years that she has left on this earth, to go about the business of living, instead of simply surviving. Basically, that's what Mom is doing, surviving. Some days I'm not sure if she is functioning; I think she's just surviving.

Louie had such a big heart. He would not want us sitting and counting the days until we are with him. I think what he said in the letter was true—we were the ones tying him to this earth. Maybe Mom is still doing it; I don't know. I haven't had any other spiritual experiences since the letter, as much as I long for them. But it truly is hard when you're trying to get your life back in order, and you see your parents and siblings suffering.

Debi, the children, my siblings, and I are talking about the happy memories; the memories bring us joy. Mom is on a journey down memory lane of destruction, because the memories are not bringing her joy; they only set her back more. I wish the Lord would have left a book down here on grief and mourning to ease this pain somehow, but I think there are some things the Lord wants us to learn on our own. That's the reason I'm trying to put this together. If it helps one person or one hundred thousand people, it would be worth it. I hope someone can find some words in this book that will help make the journey a little bit easier.

*One of the things I thought when Louie died was, "How could the sun possibly be shining?" When I think now as to how the sun could shine, it was God's beaming happiness that Louie was with him. That's what it was like when Louie was with us. It was like sunshine everyday. He brought so much to our family.

*Early on I talked about the closeness the family felt with one another after Louie died. You may find as time goes on the love remains with one another, but there comes a time where everyone pulls away a bit. More than likely it will get back to closeness again. Space allows time for healing, for working through your feelings and emotions, and people are at different phases in their grief. Allow the healing to take place; then things can get back to normal, whatever normal is for you and your family. I know it's hard to let go, even if for a while, because you already have a loved one in heaven and you don't want to be separated from your loved ones on earth. Be patient, pray, and ask for the Lord's guidance and strength to help ease your pain.

14
Beginning to Heal

*Will I ever accept Louie's death at his young age? No, I still can't accept his death after nine months. The reason I can't accept it is I don't understand it. It's hard for me to accept things in life when I don't understand why they happened. So I am working on living again. I'm learning how to live without Louie being here with us. My heart still aches, my heart still cries, my heart still says, "No, no, no," but my heart has to start learning this is how it is. I will never forget him. A day does not go by that I don't think about him, that I don't miss him. The pain is there; it's just manageable. The fact that we try to go on with our lives the best way we can does not mean that we accept a loved one's death. It means that we learn to live with it, and that's what we need to do to survive. I have to try to do this for my husband, children, and the rest of the family because, hopefully, by showing them the strength that I am trying to have, they'll find strength and go on the best way they can too. At this point, Mom's a different story, but I'm trying for the rest of the family.

*This journey is not easy. Don't ever let anyone give you the impression that it's easy; it isn't. I feel this journey is never going to end until I am reunited with Louie and my other loved ones in heaven. But with any journey you have to keep going forward if you want to be able to get to an end point. There are still days I take a step backwards. That's normal; it is going to happen. There are days that are harder to get through no matter what the reason—a song, a memory. But I must keep trying. Like any other siblings, we had a disagreement here and there, but we loved each other, and we always managed to get through things we didn't agree on. If we hurt each other, we forgave each other. That's how we were raised. That's what we know. That's what we believe.

*What still troubles me is at that July wedding, the last time we were together, Louie asked if I could take his boys the next week. I had them for a week in June. I was in the midst of redecorating the whole house, beds were down, and my boys were sleeping on the floor. The paperhangers were coming over every day. I said, "I don't have anywhere to put them. How about in a couple of weeks?" He said that would be okay. Besides good-bye and kisses, those were the last words I spoke to my brother while he was alive. How I regret it. The guilt I feel still bothers me. If I had taken the boys, maybe I would have noticed something and could have tried to get him to go to the doctor. I rarely say no. I don't know why I didn't just have the boys bring sleeping bags, but I must have been extremely overwhelmed with everything going on in the house. Learn from my mistake, so you don't have to deal with guilt for something you can't change. Live each day with your loved ones in a way that you'll feel no pain from guilt for something you didn't do.

In the beginning there were certain songs that triggered the emotions. I keep trying to find songs that will bring comfort. Some songs are difficult to listen to in their entirety without shedding a few tears. One of the songs that I still have a hard time with is bittersweet for me because it brings comfort and pain at the same time—Mariah Carey and Boyz II Men's "One Sweet Day."

Another song that in the first five or six months would break me right into tears is a song by Colin Raye entitled "Love Remains." All the memories came flooding back of the joy I know Louie brought my parents as a son when he was growing up. That song reminded me so much of Louie's life at that point. When I first heard the song, I knew his love remained with us, but I was not in any shape to make sense out of that. Now I often put that song on intentionally. It brings comfort because I know Louie's love remains with us, and no one can ever take it away. It's in me, my parents, my siblings, his wife, his children—all who knew and loved him. To us, eternity is in years, but to God and our loved ones who have died, it is a blink of God's eye, and we will be reunited, never to part again.

*When this journey began for me a little over nine months ago, one of the things I had always done since I was a teenager when something was on my mind or I was feeling sad, I would write. I would turn to the Lord as well when things were difficult or weren't going the way I'd hoped they would. Often I turned to my mother for advice. But Mom's not really the one to turn to right now. She's still trying to deal with her own grief.

At the beginning of this journey, I wasn't sure which direction I was going, what was happening exactly; many things were happening at once. It was pretty normal for me to pick up paper and pen and write although I didn't intend to write a book. These were just my words for the feelings I was experiencing at the time. One of the things I started doing in the beginning, probably within the first week or two, was going to the library and trying to find something that would give me answers and would bring peace. I found books as I explained earlier. George Anderson's *We Don't Die* is a wonderful book that talks about our relatives not really dying; they are just on the other side. That's why often you may experience a smell or have a spiritual experience related to that person. We know that it has to be them and no one else. That book brought comfort in the respect that Louie is still living. He's just not on this side of the earth. It's a different type of life for him now with the Lord.

I was searching for the answer on how you get through this grief. The more I searched, the less I found. Another book I had read was *Life after Life* by Raymond A. Moody, and then I found a video of the same title. The video brought me more comfort than the book. As I continued on this journey, and as time progressed, I was getting a better handle on my feelings. I wasn't feeling quite so disoriented. I started talking to a couple of my friends, sharing my frustration, because I couldn't find something that would give me more answers. Maybe one of the reasons I haven't found it is that I don't think there is a book that has the answers. How do you get through this journey? That's where the foundation for this book began.

In all honesty, I think there are several ways to get through this journey of unexpected grief. There are a lot of factors that can interplay, but as we continue this journey, we'll see there is no one true answer. However, there are things we can do to help make the journey through the phases of grief easier, but there is nothing that can make it go away. For example, the journey is going to be different, depending upon which loved one dies. Whether it's a mother, father, brother, grandparent, aunt, uncle, cousin, friend, or someone who simply touched your heart, the grief process is going to be different. The factors that interplay depend on the relationship you had with that person. Was it a strong and loving relationship? Or was the person someone who you simply cared about? Was your whole life focused on the needs of this person? Was the person ill? All these factors will play into one's journey. Let's say this person was someone you loved deeply, who added so much to your life, just as Louie was to ours. My grief process will be different based on all those factors.

*It's the eve of the first anniversary of Louie's passing. My emotions and feelings are on overdrive. My heart—what's left of it—aches. I feel the anticipation of what tomorrow will bring— the pain, the tears, the heartache, and reliving the day. I'm numb. Could I have actually survived an entire year without him? I wish it could have been a test of survival, and I could have him back again. Someone would say, "You proved you could survive. Good job. You can have him back in recognition of your survival."

15
Continuing to Heal

✷ It's so hard to believe that one year has come and gone since Louie's death. I awoke in the morning with tears in the corners of my eyes. Thoughts went to the year before. In some ways the year went by so quickly; in others it feels as if Louie's been away a lifetime. They say the firsts of everything are the hardest. We've gotten through the first of everything now. My heart is still broken, and it still pains me, more so today. In some respects it's easier, but I am convinced that my heart will never fully mend. It's a little easier to breathe deeper too. I know my life will never be the same. But one can survive a tremendous loss. It takes time, and while time may not heal us completely, it will ease our pain. Mom and Dad came over to spend the day; it was a comfort to be with them. We shared memories and shed tears, but we did it together. Mom is doing better. Time has eased her grief, but she will never get over the passing of her son.

*I don't think you can go through this type of experience without growing, learning, and changing; mourning is a lot of hard work. People all mourn differently. We all get through the grief process at our own pace. Once the shock begins to wear off and the reality sets in, you may think you will never come out of the grief. What I have found to be helpful is the writing I've done, describing my feelings, emotions, and experiences. When I read what I wrote about my feelings last year, I realize how much healing I've done over the year.

*I continue to mourn and grieve the passing of my brother and will for the rest of my life, but once we work through the initial stages, we learn better control. Once we work through our feelings and emotions, we can go on. Most of us are actually stronger than we believe or even realize we are.

*I shared earlier my concern for my mother. The first week of August she shared a tape with me. It was entitled "Carm's Conversation with Carm" (my mother's name). She taped it just before Mother's Day. As I listened, parts of the tape brought me to tears. If you recall, I felt one of three things might happen with my mother: (1) The Lord would allow her to see a vision, have a dream or hear Louie's voice and he would tell her to go on; (2) She would come to terms and realize how much the rest of her children and grandchildren love and need her; (3) She would go to a premature death by not taking care of herself.

My mother will never get over my brother's death, nor will she accept it, but she is trying to learn how to live with it and realizes how much we all love and need her here with us. By Mom's sharing this tape with me, I'm able to complete a journey of grief for now. I am so proud of her.

Here are some excerpts of the tape of my mother's conversations with herself:

"Carmella, I'm not telling you to stop grieving. All I'm telling you is that you've got to begin to live what years you've got left. Louie wants you to be the happy, jovial person you sometimes can be."

"Carmella, if you are going to continue to zero in

on what you have lost and forget about what you have here, you are the loser. And so will your children lose. The mother they care about is only half here."

"Love has not died. He is in heaven with our other loved ones."

I can't imagine exactly what her grief feels like. Mom has had confirmations from the Lord that Louie is with him. I'm not sure what helped Mom come to the realization of how much we love and need her, but I thank my lucky stars or whatever was shining upon us that gave my mother back for however long.

*Today Louie would have been forty-two years old. Last year on this day we buried his body. My feelings and emotions are as they've been these last few days. I've done what I can to keep myself busy. I started the day in a productive way by going to the early morning Mass and lighting a candle in memory of my love for Louie and a happy birthday. I'm actually able to hear his name in church as the Mass was said for him without breaking down in a total sob. That in itself is another step toward healing. In the journey, sometimes all you can take are baby steps toward the process of healing. We find as time goes on, the steps possibly get a little larger, and we don't seem to be stepping backwards anymore or at least not as often. This is a journey that we will continue throughout our life on this side of the earth until one day when we are reunited with our loved one.

16
Comfort Measures

L et me share with you the comfort measures I used. Some work better than others. Even if this person is one with whom your relationship wasn't strong, but you feel the hurt, the pain, the grief—these things may still work for you. I will include measures I've learned, whether I found them helpful or not, as well as things others have shared with me that they used. Just because a measure may not have benefited me, it may still give you some relief.

The first thing that I have already touched on is the writing. I would write and write and write. I could get lost in my thoughts and put down on paper exactly what I was feeling. It is not judgmental to write, but it hurts. It hurts tremendously to do this. When you put the feelings on paper, it doesn't mean they are going to go away. There may be times you will be surprised at what you write. I let my hand do the writing and my heart express the feelings. There is a difference when you are writing from your heart instead of your head. Your heart always tells it like it is; it doesn't play games with you, whereas your head may attempt to make you believe things that really are not true.

The more you write, especially in the beginning, you feel a temporary relief. As you continue writing, and time progresses, hopefully you will experience this when you read over what you have written. You'll probably cry, and you may think, as I did, where did those words come from? You don't have to share these heart feelings with anyone unless you choose to. This can be a personal journal. You may find that the more you read, the easier it gets to hear those words again. While you're writing and re-reading, you may not know at the time that you're healing.

For me the healing began at about six months, I began to read the actual feelings I had written in the early weeks of this journey. I could see on paper, as time progressed, that I was feeling stronger and beginning to heal although at the time of the writing I hadn't realized it. Writing was a big part of the healing process for me. Hopefully, as you read the words describing your feelings during the early phases of the grief process, you can also see the healing taking place. I said it before, and I'll say it again: Healing yourself from this grief and mourning does not mean you will ever forget your special person; the grief may never fully go away. In some respects the grief didn't go away completely when my other relatives died. But you do learn to live with it. That's another basis of what this journey is about—you learn how to deal with the grief and the mourning, and you learn how to continue on with your life.

Another comfort measure is drawing what you're feeling. Use the colors you're feeling. For example, red represented anger to me when drawing. Black represented emptiness; dark blue, sadness. Get a box of colored pencils, pens, markers, chalk, paints, crayons, and paper you can use for drawing. Go off by yourself, to a place you can derive the most comfort. Draw, once a day, twice a day, whatever you need. You don't have to be an artist. I have drawn a picture or two, but writing has been the best release for me. Drawing for many people is helpful. If you watch the progression of your drawings and colors, hopefully you will see the further you get into this journey of grief, the more healing is taking place. You may see the colors change from primary to pastel. In the beginning, relief may be temporary, but if it's five, ten, fifteen, thirty minutes of relief you receive, this gives your heart a chance to begin healing and your mind a chance to rest.

Here's another comfort measure I used: Within the first week or two of Louie's death, I got a picture of him with a big smile, a silly headband with springs and glittered balls, the picture from our last Christmas together. That was Louie, that was his personality. I put it in a gold frame on top of the stereo speakers, and I lit a candle. In the beginning I kept burning candles while I was home and awake. You may wonder what was the purpose. The purpose, the meaning for me, was to keep Louie's light burning. At the time, it was what I needed to do. As time goes on, when I'm writing, having a sad day, which I refer to as a candle day or simply a day when I'm missing him, I usually light candles.

I still have those kinds of days. As I have mentioned before, to me this journey is a continuous process. Don't think that when you're finished reading this book, you'll be healed. Hopefully, you will be stronger, or feel you have some idea of how to attempt to begin your journey. Even when I bring the book to a close, my journey is going to continue until I'm with my brother in heaven. But I'm going to be able to deal with the journey's difficult days, because I've allowed my heart to continue the process of healing. That's all a part of what this is about also—allowing your heart, your soul, and your body to heal. I have to tell you that you're the only one who can start this process, to continue this process. You must give yourself permission for your heart, soul, and body to heal.

Any of these comfort measures we use help us along the way—

writing, drawing, the candle. Talking to people—your friends, priest, minister, others who have gone through this—can be helpful mechanisms. But the only person who can do the actual healing is you, along with the help of God. But it's you. It's hard work, a day-to-day process that you have to work at. You can't simply go into a room and sit on a chair and say, "Okay, start healing me." It doesn't work that way. *You* have to work at healing *yourself.* The key factor on this journey is that *you* have to do the work and allow yourself to *heal.*

Let's get back to the candle. The candle has its place in the living room. Sometimes I change the holder; at times I use scented candles, depending on my mood. As time goes on I don't feel the need to burn the candle every day. Now I have a tendency to burn the candle on special days. You may remember that I said this is my way of keeping Louie's light burning. That's true. However, as I allow myself to heal, I don't need to see the light burning in the visual sense. I feel his lovelight burning in my heart, burning inside of me. Sometimes even though I can feel it in my heart when I'm sitting in the living room looking at his picture, I light the candle because I want to see the light burning. It brings me comfort.

Another comfort measure I use is in church. I light a candle once a month or so in his memory. The candle is burning in the church for him and my other relatives. That has brought me comfort to know the candle burns continuously for him in one of the Lord's earthly homes.

Another comfort measure for me is a handsome male angel statue I bought at Louie's store. I placed it with the picture and candle, because I feel that Louie has become one of God's angels, and this gives me continuous comfort. On the stereo speaker I have the picture, the candle, and the angel—all in honor and memory of my brother. Since I started this memory spot, the children have added special mementos. My son Tony brought home a small plaque from his religion class that had a beautiful rainbow on it and said "God keeps his promises." He put it near the picture. That was his contribution, and it's still there. Another day, Tony brought home a beautiful candleholder. Then Mike brought home a cross he made from twigs, and other mementos were added. Our memory place was getting so loaded that I asked the children to pick out one or two of the mementos they wanted to keep there and put the others in their rooms. It brings us comfort to be able to look at those items on a daily basis.

Since I spend a good amount of time in the kitchen on any given day, on my refrigerator I have a family picture, a picture of Louie and a picture of me sitting on Louie's lap that Mom gave me after Louie died. I was six-and-a-half months, and Louie was about five years old. The pictures bring me comfort. I often kiss the picture of Louie. Pictures for some people are comforting; for others they cause more pain. You have to make the decision for yourself whether a picture is a comfort measure or if it brings more pain.

Along the same line is watching videos of your loved one. To watch a video was very difficult in the first few months. Louie was moving, talking, and laughing, and hearing his voice was painful. As time goes on, watching the videos of him brings comfort. I'm reminded of what his voice sounds like, although I don't think I will forget. It's nice to have the videos to watch him so full of life. I still feel he is full of life; he's just in another place— heaven.

I have also found that as time goes on, talking about Louie

gets much easier—telling people what a character he was, the things he said, and the crazy things he did.

Last year, Mom told me that when Louie was setting up the walkway and an elf display at his store, his son Nicholas, who was five at the time, was hiding. He didn't know that his dad knew he was there. Louie decided to have a conversation with the elves.

Nick came around the corner and said, "Who are you talking to, Dad?"

Louie told him, "The elves."

Nick asked, "What did they say?"

Louie said, "They said they don't like you."

"That's not true, Dad. The elves can't talk."

"Yes, they can, but I told them you have to come to work with me because you're my son."

Nick told Louie that when he grows up and takes over the store, he's firing those elves. On one of the three occasions when I went to the store, Nick was there. He was walking through the display with us, and when we got to the first scene of elves, I said, "Nick, are these the elves that told Daddy they didn't like you?"

"No, Aunt Theresa, they're down here. I'll show you when we get there." I laughed so hard. His father had such a sense of humor, and Nick is so much like his dad.

Sometimes the sudden death of someone we love may be more difficult because we never had the opportunity to say goodbye. For example, when someone has cancer and is aware his or her time is limited, we have the opportunity to express our feelings to that person. It's a way of gaining closure to a death. What I still have some trouble with is not having had the chance to say goodbye, to say that *I love you* one last time to my brother. The last time I had told Louie "I love you" was at Christmastime, eight months before he died.

Maybe it was a few months or years since you told the loved one you have lost what he or she really meant to you. Sometimes it is hard because it seems it's unfinished business. It's difficult for me to try to get through this because there are things I wanted to say to Louie. What I would suggest doing to bring comfort and closure is to sit down and write a letter saying what you need to tell that person had death been expected. Even if death was expected, but you didn't say all you wanted, writing a letter to that loved one may bring comfort.

If you're the type of person who derives more comfort at the graveside, do it there. Tell or write how you feel because I believe our loved ones can hear us and are aware of our feelings although they may not be able to respond to us in a way we are used to. If one letter or conversation isn't enough, if it brings you comfort, continue until you feel you have expressed what you need to bring closure. If it is anger you are experiencing, you can do the same. Even if you don't believe you are being heard, this is still a method you can use to release the anger in a constructive manner, providing the opportunity to get relief from what you are feeling.

17
A Spiritual Experience/
More Comfort Measures

On a beautiful sunshiny day within the first month or two of Louie's death, I had windows open between the living room and dining room to get a cool breeze in the house. I was trying to go about the business of doing my daily chores. I don't know if it was a song, a sound, a memory, but something struck me. I broke down, the tears came, I was saying, *I don't understand why this happened* and *I love you, Louie. Do you know I love you? Do you know how much I miss you?* I put myself in the corner of the dining room, brought my legs to my chest and curled up into a ball, and put my head on my knees and cried. After a few minutes, the glass pieces of the chandelier starting swaying and clanging. It was enough of a clang that I stopped crying and looked up at the chandelier and said, " Is that you, Louie?" I think it was his way of letting me know that he is okay and that he knows how we feel. Even though he didn't say it verbally, he got my attention. I have not had that type of experience—an actual vision or had him speak to me—except for that evening with Mike, and Mike was the one who heard what he was saying.

There are many other things that people do to find comfort. An example is planting a tree, a special rosebush, or flower in memory of that person we love so much. These things can be done as a tribute.

Another great comfort measure for me is prayer. Prayer can bring comfort. Praying is something I've done on a daily basis, along with my daily rosary, for quite some time. Some days I would say two and three rosaries. It gave my mind some relief. I have found that the more time I spend on constructive thoughts and activities, the more time my brain, my body, and my soul have a chance to heal. What better way to heal than through prayer? Pray alone, pray with someone, but pray.

These are a few of the things that I did and still continue to do. I use these different comfort measures because I still need comfort. I will need comfort for the death of my Louie for the rest of my life. You may also need comfort with the death of your loved one. This isn't something that we ever get over. I think if you tell yourself it's over, you're through grieving, you may be trying to fool yourself. You may find that you have never fully grieved. So grief accumulates. It has a way of catching up with you. You never escape it. You can never escape going through the grief process. If you try to delay it, and you wear the "everything is okay mask," as long as I did, going through the process becomes even more difficult. Sometimes the process can take longer than if you had made an attempt to deal with what you were feeling one day at a time, one hour at a time, one minute at a time.

Although I've cautioned against wearing it too long, the mask of "Everything is okay...everything is fine...I'm fine...life is still good...life is still wonderful" can serve as a comfort measure. In the beginning it benefited me because I was so overwhelmed with grief that to let my true feelings out at once probably would have shattered me. It was helpful to be able to wear the mask when the children were home. The mask is a comfort measure that I would suggest using in the beginning and then intermittently because as time goes on you need to deal with your feelings. But the more I wore the mask, the harder it was for me to get through the grief. I didn't think I would ever get to a point where I would be able to take the mask off. I was afraid to take it off. I feared if I needed it again I may not be able to put it back on, and then I would have to look my true self in the mirror and deal with what I was feeling.

Wearing the mask is extremely tiring. I didn't think I would ever have a day where I could be free of the mask. I would say that after nine months of this journey, I am free of that mask. I now realize that I wasted more energy wearing the mask for as long as I did than if I would have dealt with the feelings as they were coming, even if it was at a slow pace. Once I learned to allow myself to experience the feelings as they came, I no longer needed to wear the mask.

It is important to give yourself permission to cry if you need to. Give yourself permission to laugh. Give yourself permission to spend time with others and try to enjoy yourself, whether it is for an hour or two or an entire evening. Whatever it is you need at that time, give yourself permission to do that. Also, remember that if you go out and you find you don't want to be there, give yourself permission to go home. Remember that on your journey through grief, be it expected or unexpected grief, give yourself permission to do what you need at that time. Always keep in mind, if a practice brings you comfort and it doesn't hurt you or anyone else, if it's not destructive in any way, then do it.

Another comfort measure is putting together a scrapbook. I have begun to compile newspaper articles and memorabilia about Louie. I'm going to set time aside to put an "In Loving Memory of Louie" scrapbook together. When I had the time earlier, I didn't have the desire or motivation to do it. It would have been too painful. When I finally do have the time, I know it will bring comfort, and I'm hoping the tears I shed will be tears of loving memories and not tears of pain.

Here's another comfort measure that I have not been able to do but one that you may find very comforting: Take an article of clothing such as a sweater or shirt and put some of your loved one's favorite cologne on the clothing and wear it around the house. Colleen shared this with me and said she found great comfort in the familiarity of her dad's sweater with the scent of his cologne. Especially in the beginning, she wore it everyday.

Another terrific comfort for me are my cats, Nicky and Max. I think animals have a sixth sense when people feel sad or are having a difficult day. In the beginning, when I was so depressed and feeling so sad, my cats, especially Nicky, could always sense it. He would climb on my lap and rub his furry face against my face as if he was trying to wipe away the tears that were ever present on my cheeks. He would follow me from room to room, and when I was crying, he would rub around my legs to get my attention. It was comforting to pick him up and hear him purr, to feel that soft fur on my hands when I held him and cried. If you are alone, maybe you would like to consider a pet. I would recommend a kitten. I love all animals, but the reason I suggest a kitten is that they don't require too much work, and when you are so down, it is hard to take care of yourself, let alone an active puppy. But on the other hand, if you're not a cat lover, waiting until you get stronger and getting a puppy may be the diversion you need to rest your mind and bring your spirits up. Animals are so free about giving love, and they enjoy getting love in return.

A hobby can also be a comfort. Mine is painting ceramics.

I've had this hobby for about twelve years. However, I admit that I didn't start painting again until somewhere between six and nine months after Louie died. But since I've started again, I paint as often as I can. I find it to be very relaxing. If you like, try your hobby, and if you don't have one, try to start one. Depending on what you choose, a hobby can also be a way of getting out among people again.

Imagery is another comfort measure that I was able to use for short periods of time. Imagery is a way of trying to relax and to bring comfort. I would imagine that I was in another place. For me, lying on the beach in the sand with the sun shining on my face was what I would imagine. Or another image was walking on the beach in the evening with the sun setting and the moon rising, hearing the quiet sounds of nature. Try to imagine a place or experience that brings you the most comfort.

The final comfort measure that I used, at six weeks and six months after Louie died, was the bereavement support group. I found comfort in knowing that people understood the pain I was feeling; I could be myself. I could cry, laugh, or just listen. You may want to check with your local funeral homes, hospitals, and/or churches for the availability of such groups in your neighborhood. Don't be ashamed to go to a support group. In the beginning, I thought if I went to this group it was a sign of weakness, that I needed to try to be strong. At one time or another, we all need others to help us. If you're uncomfortable with a group of people you don't know, you may want to consider going to a therapist who specializes in bereavement counseling. Asking for help is not a sign of weakness; it is an act of courage and a show of strength. Listening to others' stories, while no one can say their pain is worse than someone else's, can help you realize you're not the only one going through this journey; awareness of that in itself can bring comfort.

If none of the above comfort measures are working for you, a final suggestions is simply to try diversions. Reading was a big diversion for me; I could get lost in a novel and forget what I was feeling for short periods at a time. Go for a walk, garden, straighten out a drawer, phone a friend, rent a comical video, take a drive, go for ice cream, go to the movie theatre, buy yourself something—the list could go on.

Your hobby may also be used as a diversion. Try to do whatever will bring you comfort because you deserve it. And even if these are simply diversions, they will give your mind a chance to rest and continue the process of healing.

As I'm reading over some of the writing I did yesterday and earlier, to see where I want to start today, my voice is shaking. The tears are sliding down my face. Today is a candle day. It's been just over a year. See, I bet you thought I was done with that. No, on some days I'm stronger than others, but today is a candle day. I lit a candle next to his picture on the stereo and one next to me. You may have days like this too, but don't feel bad; do what you need to have a productive day and move on. Seeing the light flicker next to me brings me comfort, so I can continue on this journey and try to help others on their journey too.

So where do we go from here? Are you still wondering what is normal? Are you still convinced you will never feel joy in your heart again? Are you still having days where you want to die? Do you always cry when you hear a certain song? Do you often feel as though you want to shout, "Stop the world! I want to get off!"? Do you still wonder how you are going to get through tomorrow? If you are still answering yes to most of the questions, that's okay. I've been on this journey for a year and a couple weeks, and some days my answers are still yes to some of the questions. If you remember, I mentioned earlier that I feel this is a journey that continues on in life; for most, it is not something we will complete on this side. But let us take one step at a time.

18
Stages of Grief:
Normal versus Abnormal

Without getting technical, let me share some of the normal feelings you may or may not experience. Let's begin with the stages of grief/crisis/tragedy, according to the well-known book, *On Death and Dying* by Elisabeth Kubler-Ross:

1. Denial
2. Anger
3. Bargaining
4. Depression
5. Acceptance

You may or may not experience all of these stages, and you may return to a previous stage before you work through them entirely. Some people may never be able to accept the death of a loved one. I can't accept the fact that Louie is no longer here, but there are a lot of things in life I can't accept. But I am learning how to live without Louie being here with me. If that's the best I can do, then so be it. It is a way of moving on instead of being stuck in this tornado of grief.

The following are the feelings I experienced when Louie died; some I still experience:

Anger—because he was gone so quickly…because he hadn't taken care of himself. He didn't eat properly or exercise, and he was a smoker.

Anxiety—because of the whole crisis/tragedy

Denial—when I found he died, I kept saying the hospital must have made a mistake

Fatigue—from not being able to sleep…my mind on over-drive all the time

Fear—that I would never feel any type of normalcy in my life again

Guilt—for the feelings I was experiencing, feeling I wasn't giving my husband and boys my full attention

Helplessness—not knowing what to do…how to give the comfort Mom and the family needed as well as comfort myself

Longing—to be with Louie either here or in heaven (then guilt again for feeling that way)

Losing it—the pain of grief was so intense I felt as if the line between sane/insane crossed each other

Numbness—because I was afraid to feel the pain for fear I couldn't cope with it

Regret—for not taking Louie's boys the week he asked me to.

Reproach—I told myself that I was the nurse…somehow I should have known that something was wrong

Sadness—that he was gone…that his wife lost her husband and the children lost their father

Sensitivity—able to cry at the drop of a hat

Shock—that he could actually be gone…that he died from a heart attack

You may experience the same feelings, but your reasons may be different. Also, the list may not be totally inclusive. You may have experienced feelings not listed, and this doesn't mean they are abnormal.

The following are other normal feelings you may experience; although I have not experienced them myself. These are feelings that others told me they experienced. By becoming aware of these, you will have an idea of other feelings you may experience and realize that they are not abnormal.

Confusion—what to do next...can't seem to put thoughts in proper perspective

Despondency—feeling everything is hopeless

Disorganization—no matter how hard you try, you cannot seem to put things in proper order

Freedom— maybe your loved one was very ill, and you were the primary caregiver

Loneliness—if it was just two of you and now you're left alone

Panic—how can you survive without your loved one

Relief—after a long illness, your loved one is out of pain

Resentment—that your loved one left you, whether it was his or her choice to make or not

Worthlessness—without your loved one, you are nothing...that person added so much to your life

Chapter 19
Physical Symptoms and Behaviors of Grief: Normal versus Abnormal

Next let's address the normal physical symptoms you may feel. These are the symptoms that I experienced:

- Crying
- Exhaustion
- Insomnia
- Loss of weight
- Nausea/vomiting
- Sighing
- Emptiness
- Heart palpitations
- Loss of appetite
- Lump in the throat
- Shortness of breath
- Weakness

These are normal symptoms I did not experience, but others shared with me that they did:

- Dry mouth
- Isolation
- Overeating
- Searching for something to do
- Increased interest in sex

- Loss of interest in sex
- Restlessness
- Sleepiness

Normal behaviors of grief that I experienced:
- Association with deceased's objects—I carry a family picture, Louie's store picture, and his memorial card in my purse
- Dreaming of Louie
- Going places—to his store; this made me feel more of a connection to him
- Grief assault—breakdown into unprovoked tears
- Inability to concentrate
- Withdrawing from social activities

Normal behaviors of grief that I did not experience:
- Avoidance—of items or places that will remind you of your loved one
- Overdoing—activities or thoughts until you're too tired to go on
- Treasuring—items that belong to your loved one
- Fidgeting—unable to sit still

Abnormal feelings of grief would be the following:
- Becoming dependent on over-the-counter or prescription drugs
- Becoming dependent on alcohol to deal with your feelings and emotions
- Feeling such severe depression that you are unable to function with basic everyday tasks

•Obsessing about death or making plans on how to kill
yourself so that you can be with your loved one

If you should experience any of the above and cannot shake the feeling, get help immediately. Call your doctor, priest or pastor, or 9-1-1, whichever is appropriate for you at the time.

Other suggestions that may be helpful:

Many bereavement counselors suggest postponing any major decisions for at least a year. For instance, I wanted to quit my job and do something else. It's a year later, and in some ways I still feel it is time for me to move on. Now would be an appropriate time because I waited the year. So if it is at all possible, try to postpone decisions such as changing jobs or buying a new home until you are able to think a little more clearly.

As difficult as it is, especially in the beginning, try to eat foods that are nutritious and to avoid overeating.

Try to exercise, even if just by taking a walk in your own yard for a short period of time.

Try to rest during the day if you need to, and sleep at night whatever amount is adequate for you.

Confide in someone you trust, and express what you are feeling.

For some people who are grieving, leaving all objects and clothing in their customary places, or leaving objects where your loved one had placed them last can be very comforting. This was not something I needed to think about; the objects I have that Louie had given me would not be anything I would consider getting rid of. Colleen shared that at first, after her dad died, it was a comfort to go to her parents' home and see her dad's glasses on the table where he had always kept them. After about a month or two, her mom moved them to the dresser in the bedroom, and now they are with some of his other belongings—his comb, brush, key ring—in the top drawer of his dresser. Colleen's mom did donate some of his clothing, but the rest remains in his earthly space.

For other people in grief, removing the personal belongings of their loved one and either putting them away or getting rid of everything brings them the most comfort. When I stayed with my sister-in-law Debi that first week after Louie died, she was cleaning and sorting through much of his belongings. As I stood there and watched her throw away things such as his toothbrush and razor, I thought to myself, *I would have been saving it all*. I even thought about taking a few of the things out of the garbage can when she wasn't looking. She sorted through and got rid of all his work clothes because she said she felt that part of the reason he was no longer here was that he worked too hard. Debi must have read my mind because she said, "If I thought saving all this stuff would bring him back, I would keep it, but it won't, so there is no sense in saving it all." At the time, standing there and watching as she threw away many of my brother's belongings was very difficult for me. Now, of course, I realize that was what she needed to do at the time, and it was her right. That's what a lot of this grief process is about—doing what is best for you so that you can get through this period. Be sure. If you are uncertain of what you want to do, then do nothing. You don't want to be sorry for something you may have done or given away in haste, anger, or denial.

20
Final Thoughts

We are nearing the thirteen-month point. As I read over and contemplate some of the things I've shared with you, I need to bring you up to date on some of the discoveries I've made. One of the things I said earlier was that I would look in a mirror and see something was missing—the sparkle put there by my brother. That is still missing, but let's take this a little farther. As I mentioned, I kept trying to get back to the person I was. I didn't feel the same way. I wanted some normalcy in my life again. I have learned I'm not the same person I was before my Louie died. How can I be? His death has changed me. Someone who was a very important part of my life is no longer here.

I also shared that I felt I had so little control over my life, and I didn't like that. Well, let's start with that point first. There is a lot in this world that we don't have control over. Death of a loved one is one of the many things. I don't feel I need control of everything that goes on around me, but I need to feel that there are at least parts of my life I can control. I feel that is why I kept making so many changes in the beginning and went round and round in a circle of nowhere. I was trying to control things that are uncontrollable. What I needed to realize was that I had to take control of things in my life that were controllable. For example, this may seem silly, but I have been cleaning and organizing rooms in my house for the last few months, accomplishing some of the changes I have wanted to make for quite a while but never took the time to get them done. The way my home is kept is something I can control. I realize it is a minor aspect of my life to gain control over, but when you think about it, how much in life can we say we have control of ? We can control the way we feel and treat others. We have no control of how others feel about us, or the way they treat us and so on. So through organizing and cleaning, I have achieved control of one aspect of my life. Furthermore, this has made me feel better because the organized appearance of my home gives me a feeling of satisfaction. I don't feel as disoriented and over-whelmed as I did in the beginning. Once things are in their proper places, it's very easy to keep my home organized. This allows me more free time.

I have learned that I am not the same person I was before Louie died. I don't feel someone can go through a major devastating crisis and come out being the person he or she was. I have changed. I feel that a small piece of me, from my heart, went with my Louie, and that is the part of me that made me who I was when I was with him. But that's okay. If that part went with Louie, I believe that it must be the part he needed to take with him to make his journey complete—to make him feel as if we are still together.

In many respects, I have grown, because I have learned from this experience. Although I knew before how precious life is, this experience has reinstilled in me that we must never take life for granted. We must never take someone's love for granted. A loved one can literally be here today and gone tomorrow. It has reinstilled in me the importance of spending quality time with those I love. It has reminded me how important it is to tell those we love how we truly feel about them. It has also reminded me how important it is not to waste time on life's trivialities, but to focus on what we feel for one another—to hug, kiss, and love one another as if it's the last time we will see them. My love for Louie is still in my heart; it will be forever. I will miss and think about him every day, but I know he wants me to go on until we are reunited.

I have experienced that once you begin to get accustomed to the changes in yourself and address your feelings and continue healing, "normalcy" will return. It is a different normal because your loved one isn't there any longer. Eventually, we return to the business of living, unless we choose to stay stuck in the early phases of the grief process. It is by no means easy to do this, but when I needed to, I returned to the one-day, one-hour, one-minute philosophy. One step at a time, until I was comfortable with the "new normal".

Although we know we are on this journey of grief, other family members and friends know also. However, the rest of the world does not. By this I mean that life will continue with the positive and negative it has to offer. Other happenings in our life will continue and possibly another crisis we have to deal with when we are in the midst of this journey. Or some of the little irritations life can bring may get in the way of the grief process. Your grief process can be changed or altered temporarily. Once you deal with your new situation, your journey will pick up again.

Perhaps you may have also taken a few steps backwards, but that's okay. I suggest you do the best you can to get back on track and attempt to continue working toward healing. Remember, if you sweep your feelings under the carpet, in six months, a year, or five years, they will catch up with you again. Then you may have to start all the way at the beginning again, and you surely don't want to do that, especially since you have worked so hard to come through the beginning of the grief process.

I wish I had a magic recipe that I could give you either to heal you or to ease your pain as you travel on this journey toward healing. But I don't think it is part of our Lord's plan. I don't know the reason that we must lose someone we love and then feel the pain and the grief of the loss.

I don't know why some of our loved ones are aware their time is limited, and we are allowed to say our I love you's and our goodbyes one last time, or why other loved ones are taken without any warning. I don't know why some passages are without pain and very peaceful, or why some people suffer so before they leave us. I don't know why my Louie died. But I do know that no matter how much you love someone, how much you need someone, there are no guarantees of how long they will be with us. I also know that my love is with my Louie, and his love remains in my heart.

Today brings us to thirteen months of travel on this journey through unexpected grief. I still feel the ache of his passing. I still feel the emptiness. My heart and my head are still trying to accept the reality of Louie's not being with us any longer. I may not ever accept this loss, but I have been learning to live with it as a day-to-day process, and there are still days when I miss him terribly.

I continue to rely on my comfort measures to help me through the difficult days. If anyone had told me eleven or twelve months ago that I would write a book to help ease the pain of others on their journey, I would never have believed it. Twelve months ago I was in the midst of this tornado and didn't believe I'd ever find my way out, and I doubted if there was a way out.

Many things have changed since my Louie's death. Change is something we must learn to deal with along this journey. But I hope that you can see that the different comfort measures that I used are all means to a continuation of this journey. For me, they have been useful, and I hope that they will help to ease your pain during your journey. As time goes on, you may not feel the need to rely on comfort measures as often. But know they are there if you need them.

My most important comfort measure has been our Lord, for without him I would have never come as far as I am today. I realize now that he was always there and was my strength even when I thought he had left me alone. He carried me on the days that I just couldn't walk. And he held me on the days when I thought I would cross over the line to insanity. He sat with me on the days and nights when I put these words into the computer and thought that my heart would break completely in half. He encouraged me to remove the mask and to continue sharing my feelings, even when I was trying so hard to bury them. Without his guidance and support, I could never have completed this book. And while my journey through grief is not complete, nor is the acceptance of my Louie's death, I realize now that my life is not over, nor is my Louie's. We are physically in two different places, but our love is with each other, as a piece of my heart is with him. We have two different journeys we each must complete until we can be together again. I guess I was never able to find a book that would help me with this journey because it was part of the Lord's plan that I would take this journey and write a book to help myself and perhaps to help others. I so wish I could tell you that tomorrow you will wake up and find this was all a nightmare, and your loved one really isn't gone. I wish I could tell myself that too. But I can't. I wish I could tell you that this journey is easy and that you will be out of this pain in just a few short months. But I can't tell you that either. I wish I could be there to walk with you through the beginning of this grief. But I can't do that either, because your grief will be different from mine.

I can tell you, however, that if you take one day, one hour, one minute at a time, and even if you use baby steps, you will be able to move in the direction of healing. It's hard work, and it's very tiring. With the help of our Lord, you can initiate this grief process. You can begin this journey, and you can work toward healing; you can have your life back again. It may be different; I doubt that you're the same person you were before your loved one died.

You can find beauty in your life again. You can find meaning in your life again. And while the joy that your loved one brought may no longer be in your heart, you can find joy from your old and new friends in your life. It is possible, because I have done it as I continue to work toward complete healing. Be kind to yourself, be gentle with yourself, be understanding of yourself, and most of all, give yourself permission to heal. Ask for help if you need it. Take strength in knowing that you're not alone in what you're experiencing. The Lord is always there. The Lord has faith in you, and so do I. With the Lord all things are possible. You can do it. Begin today. Begin slowly, but begin. Take that baby step toward healing. One day you'll realize you are actually saying your loved one's name without breaking into sobs, and you will see and feel the healing taking place. You can do it. Remember, in a blink of God's eye we will be reunited with our loved ones, and what a glorious celebration that will be!

21
Other Stories of Grief

I'd like to share with you additional grief experiences and my feelings in cases of deaths that were more or less expected. The first three were family members, and the last two were family members of my friends.

Grandma Toon, my mother's mom, lived with Tony, our son Tony, and me for a month in March 1984. Mom had her dream vacation planned to Rome, Italy, before Grandma got ill. Mom was going to cancel her trip, but Tony and I had said we'd bring her to our home since I wasn't working. Besides, we lived in a one-floor ranch and Grandma would be able to get her wheelchair around easily. Mom went to Italy and had a wonderful time, but when she got back, Grandma was ill again and went back in the hospital.

I remember too well that day in March. I was trying to keep myself busy doing a good job painting the closet in Grandma's room, getting it ready for her to come home. The phone rang. It was Mom. Grandma had taken a turn for the worse. As I drove that seemingly infinite twenty minutes, a million things went through my mind. It was inconceivable to me that Grandma could really be dying. We had grown even closer while she lived with us.

I reached the hospital to find we weren't allowed in the room. Those horrible words *Code Blue* kept blaring out over and over. Her heart had stopped; they brought her back only to stick her on a ventilator. As she was rushed down the hall to ICU (Intensive Care Unit), I barely got to look at her. I was so angry. The tears rolled down my face. I threw my purse and coat against the wall.

Mom, Auntie, and I were quiet as we headed for the elevators. After waiting for I don't know how long, we were allowed to see her. She looked so pale and in pain. Machines and monitors were everywhere; her arms were even restrained. As we entered the room, someone said, "Five minutes." My grandmother is dying, and they're telling us five minutes. I went up and kissed her and told her I loved her. She looked at me with those pain-filled eyes and moved her eyes down to her hands. The tears welled in my eyes, and I said, "I can't, Grandma, I can't." I knew exactly what she wanted me to do: untie her hands so she could pull the ventilator out. (The nurse said she had pulled it out once, and that's why they restrained her hands.) I was selfish. I didn't want to let her go. As time went on and she slowly began losing consciousness, I decided to stay the night. I went home, took a shower, washed my hair, and changed clothes. My thoughts kept changing from *This is it* to *She has to pull through.* I kissed my husband and baby and told them I'd see them in the morning.

I arrived back at the hospital, and there was no change. Everyone left but Aunt Chris and me. We could visit every hour but only for five minutes. I went in before I settled into a chair in the waiting room. About eleven o'clock, one o'clock, and again at three o'clock there was no change. Her eyes were open but gave no reaction even as I spoke to her. Back in the waiting area, something woke me before 5:00 A.M. I went into the room. There was no apparent change to me, but the nurse asked me to step out. A few minutes later the nurse came and said, "I think you'd better come into the room." I told Auntie we should go to the room.

When I got to Grandma's room, the nurse said, "Your grandmother is dying. Tell her what you want; the hearing is the last to go." As the numbers on the monitors kept dropping, I immediately went to Grandma's side. Her eyes were open, staring straight ahead, as if she saw something beyond me. I grabbed her hand, leaned very close to her, and said, "Grandma, it's me, Theresa. I love you," as I choked back the tears, I thought to myself *You have to be strong now.* "Grandma, look for the light. See the light, follow the light. Now see Jesus' arms are open wide for you. Don't fight it. Go with Jesus, Grandma. I love you." I'm not sure why I said *don't fight it* because Grandma had no fear of dying. I stepped back so that Auntie could get next to her. In moments, she was gone. A doctor came and, without warning, closed her beautiful, blue eyes. That was too final for me. I stumbled backwards. We were asked to leave the room. I went to call Mom.

When we returned, the equipment was gone. Grandma looked at peace. My head told me that she was with Jesus, but my heart couldn't accept the fact at that moment. Then Mom arrived, and we all cried. We left the room and headed to the elevators. I was numb. She was gone; she was really gone. I got home, went into the house, and Tony held me. The baby was still asleep. As I walked down the hall, Grandma's bedroom door was closed. I stopped a moment, opened the door, and went in the room. The afghan she used to keep her legs warm was on the bed. I picked it up and brought it to my nose. It had her scent on it. I sobbed into it.

The next day was the wake. The afternoon was for immediate family; we would receive visitors that evening and the next day.

When I entered the funeral home, I felt a rush of emotions. *I can't make it through this... she can't really be gone this is too final... she is at peace.* When I walked into the room, I was alone with her body. I approached the casket, kissed her forehead, touched her hand. She was so cold; the life was out of her. I began crying again. I stood at the casket as if I was protecting her; I was supposed to take care of her, and I felt I had failed. The rest of the family arrived. Louie came up to me and asked me to sit down, and I cried in his arms. The rest of the services are mostly a blur. I merely went through the motions.

I felt so empty, so alone. I couldn't sleep at night. The doctor gave me a prescription for a mild tranquilizer to take at bedtime. I kept thinking I was going to die soon too. I had dreams at night of Grandma with her arms open, me running toward her, and my mom behind me screaming, "No, Mom, don't take her. She's too young. It's not her time yet. She has so much to do." Just as I was ready to reach Grandma's arms, she withdrew them and waved goodbye. I would awake with a drenched pillow as the tears continued to roll down my face. Over the months, I was so angry with God for taking her and kept questioning her happiness. I never doubted she was with Jesus. Why would I doubt her happiness? About five months after her death, Jesus answered my prayers. I dreamed about Grandma...well, it didn't feel like a dream.

Mom, Anita, Aunt Chris, my baby Tony, and I were in a little town. I said it would be nice if Christ would let us see Grandma. As we looked into a very blue sky, a luminous white castle with a white flag appeared. We started to run toward the castle. Grandma was on the left side of the door. She and Mom began to hug. We kissed, and then we were in the middle of a street. I said it wasn't enough time. Once again the castle appeared.

I said, "Grandma are you happy?"

"Yes, honey, I'm very happy."

"But Grandma, you look so tired."

"That's because I'm very busy, honey."

While Mom and Grandma continued to talk, I went for a walk. I ended up in a classroom and thought this must be where the children whom God has called home gather to learn.

I called out, "Jesus, where are you? I want to talk to you." I called out again but nothing.

When I returned, I asked Grandma, "Do you know when we write to you?"

"Yes, honey, I do."

"Do you know when we're sad and cry, when we miss you?"

"Yes, I do."

"Grandma, can you come down to earth and sit with us even if we don't know you are there?" No response. "Grandma, did you hear what I asked?"

"I'm sorry, honey, I can't answer that for you." Then I woke up. I tried desperately to fall back to sleep, but it was hopeless. This wasn't like any dream I've ever had. I felt as if I was with my Grandma. The interesting part is that as I shared this beautiful experience with Mom and described it in detail, Mom questioned me about the color of the castle and flag. Mom had always taught us that sometimes Christ speaks to us in dreams.

After this spiritual experience, I gained the peace and closure I needed to continue with my life. I knew Grandma was all right, and while I've had dreams of her since, this experience I have never felt again. I was with her. I know she's with the Lord. My heart has mended.

Now I know my Louie is with her. I know how much happiness he brought her on the earth, and I'm sure he continues to do so in paradise. I still miss her and always will. Her picture remains on the window ledge above my kitchen sink. I know that someday we will be reunited in heaven.

In January 1990 Mom called to say that she and Dad were taking Grandpa, Dad's father, to the doctor. His skin had turned yellow. Grandpa was admitted to the hospital, and this was another difficult time, although it was no surprise. Obviously, there was a problem with his liver; the rest remained to be seen. The nursing care left a lot to be desired. Grandpa spoke broken English, so there was a definite language barrier. We decided to take Grandpa home and keep him as comfortable as possible. We decided to take shifts to give him twenty-four hour care ourselves, except for the nursing requirements.

I usually took the night shift every other day. Grandpa's skin color was so yellow, he was weak, and his appetite was decreasing. A few more days and nights passed. When the tests were complete, the diagnosis was liver cancer. We would keep Grandpa as comfortable as possible. The doctors gave him about a month to live. Aunt Anita took a leave of absence from work. She would continue to be his primary caregiver, and the rest of us would continue helping.

I went over as often as possible. I figured if I stayed, God wouldn't let him die with me there; after all, I had been through this with Grandma. That was foolish, but when you're in crisis, you don't think clearly. Grandpa was in a great deal of pain. After a few heated conversations with the doctor, he prescribed a medication to be given by injection. Aunt Anita would give it; she was our nurse. When it didn't appear to help, we called the doctor, and he increased the dose. Grandpa must have been having some kind of reaction. He would sleep a short period of time and wake up thrashing his head back and forth until we could calm him. We prayed the rosary, and Auntie and I went to Mom and Dad's on the next street to sleep.

Anita, Marie, Joe, and Dad stayed with Grandpa. Early the next morning Dad came over and said, "You better go and relieve Anita and Marie. They were up all night." When Auntie and I got there, he seemed calmer, probably exhausted. The day was pretty uneventful. That night, Auntie and I stayed. She told me she'd take the first shift, so I went to bed about midnight. I woke up about three o'clock and told Auntie to get some rest. I checked on Grandpa. No change. He was still unconscious with his eyes closed. I sat in the chair across from his bed for a little while; then something told me to get closer. I took a chair from the kitchen and pulled it up next to his bed. I stroked his hair and sang songs quietly. This seemed to relax him.

At about 5:30 A.M. I noticed his respirations were decreasing, from twenty-four to twelve over a few minutes. I woke Auntie and told her I felt his time was close. We began talking to Grandpa and telling him, "Look for the light. Jesus is waiting for you." We told him that we loved him, and Auntie told him, "See your mother. Go to your mother. She is waiting for you." Grandpa opened those beautiful, blue eyes, looked beyond us at that last moment, and took the first of his last two breaths. Auntie and I started to cry, hugging each other. Grandpa, too, went home to Jesus. I called Mom and Dad. When they came over, we managed to contact the funeral home and got the living room back in order before Grandma May woke up.

The funeral is pretty much a blur. I read a poem at the end of Mass, and my sister Anita read a poem at the graveside that she had written about Grandpa. Anita shared that at Christmas Grandpa was looking around at all his great-grandchildren and said in that wonderful Italian accent, "Yeah, she's a gonna be my lasta Christmas."

Anita said, "Oh, don't say that, Grandpa." Little did we realize at the time, he was right.

Even though Grandpa was almost ninety-eight, letting him go was hard. He added so much to our lives. I felt sad, but I didn't have as difficult a time as I had when Grandma died. I cried a lot. I missed him terribly. Shortly thereafter, the wonderful memories flooded my thoughts. He was a remarkable man—a kind, loving, small in stature Italian man who lived a good Christian life. There is no doubt he is in heaven. Any time I think of Grandpa, it is with happy memories. I miss him, but I know we will be reunited in heaven.

In October 1994, I called my cousin Gina to say that Aunt Anita was not doing well. She was weak, in a great deal of pain, and having difficulty walking. Until recently, Auntie had beaten breast cancer. I met Gina at the hospital. After Auntie's MRI, the ER doctor asked to speak with me and said the cancer had spread. I don't know how to read x-rays, but I could not believe my eyes when I saw a tumor between each vertebrae, and one in her hip. The hip didn't surprise me because of the pain, but the x-ray of the spine left me speechless.

I went to tell Gina and Auntie what the doctor had said. I think Auntie knew. We decided to transfer her to another hospital. While Gina was out of the room, the doctor came in and said she wasn't anticipating any problems but wanted to discuss her wishes should a problem arise. Auntie's wishes were that there would be no extraordinary means, no CPR, ventilators, or feeding tubes. Things were moving so quickly that it wasn't all registering. After a week, she was discharged and brought to her Aunt Hazel's by ambulance on Friday. I worked the weekend, the night shift. After resting on Monday, I phoned Mom. She said that Dad had gone to visit Auntie (his sister) and kept going outside because he couldn't listen to her cries of pain. When I had talked to Gina last, Auntie was all right.

When I phoned Gina, she began to cry when she heard my voice. She said that Auntie was in a great deal of pain and seemed to be struggling to breathe, as well as having periods of apnea. That morning, Auntie had been using the walker but by evening was too weak to get out of bed.

I told her I'd be there as soon as possible. I phoned Mom so that we could go together. I told Tony what was happening, made arrangements for the boys for morning, packed an overnight bag, and was on my way. As Mom and I drove out, we had mixed emotions. We felt that Auntie might go home to Jesus that night. I wasn't ready. We prayed together and silently, feeling drawn to look toward the light; in the dark sky we saw a very bright light. It followed us for a couple of miles and then disappeared. We never did figure out what it was.

I felt a very strong presence of Grandpa—a cool breeze through the car and then a warming. When we arrived at Aunt Hazel's, I went in to see Auntie. She looked uncomfortable and exhausted. She had a morphine PCA (patient controlled analgesia) pump with a continuous infusion for pain. I settled into a chair next to Auntie's bed and suggested Gina lie next to her mom. She, too, looked exhausted. We dozed on and off during the night. Auntie was having apneic periods, but for the most part she seemed comfortable. The thought that Auntie could be dying was on my mind, although I wanted to deny it.

In the morning I was relieved. Auntie had made it through the night. I was also exhausted. I had four days with little sleep, and when you're that tired, it's difficult to think clearly. Gina and I had talked and decided it was time to get hospice involved. I handled the business calls to give Gina more time with her mom. Later that morning, family began to arrive with food and to lend support.

When I finally reached Colleen, I began to cry from relief, total exhaustion, and simple emotion. She couldn't understand what I was saying. I calmed down and told her. She said that she'd take care of the boys. I called work and asked for a leave of absence. Since I was in orientation, this wasn't a problem.

Before long, supplies arrived from hospice, including the hospital bed. None too soon, for when I sat next to Auntie the day before, the bottom of the bed broke. Gina broke the other side, so now the whole bottom of the bed was on the floor. As a team, we moved Auntie to a more comfortable position in the new bed.

Mom, Tony, and the family convinced me to go home that night to rest. It was a struggle, but I listened. (Gina later told me how nervous she was when I left her. I wish she had said something. I never would have gone.) I'd see the boys, get the house organized, pack more of my things, and return the next day. Marie would go in the morning. Mom would stay the night with Gina.

After I left, Gina said Auntie called her in the room and said, "Don't leave me alone. When he comes again, I want you to meet him." Gina asked who he was, but Auntie never answered.

When I returned the next day, Louie came out. It was such a heartwarming experience. I walked in the room, gently shook Aunt

Anita, and said, "Auntie, Louie's here." She became so totally awake and extended her arms to him and called him by his nickname "Butchie," as the tears welled in her eyes. They embraced, and my heart was so light that Louie could bring her that much comfort. I left the room so that they could be alone. By this time, I think Aunt Anita knew she was going home to the Lord.

I wish I had read Maggie Callanan's *Final Gifts* before Auntie died. I would have handled her death differently. For example, when Auntie said, "I'm coming" during one of her talking states, I said, "Where are you going? You're not going anywhere." I would have responded only, "Where are you going?" leaving her an opportunity to tell us more if she chose to, especially if she was experiencing seeing loved ones from beyond. Anyway, Louie came out of the room and said they had spent time talking. It was interesting that shortly after he left, she aroused for short periods but returned to sleeping most of the time.

That night Aunt Theresa stayed with Gina, Aunt Hazel, and me. While Aunt Theresa was sitting with Auntie, Gina and I sat in the living room and talked about where the restlessness could be coming from. We had given her permission to go home to Jesus when she was ready. A few people who hadn't been out to see Auntie would be coming within the next day or so. As the day drew to a close, Gina and I settled into the room for the night. I settled into a chair next to the bed and told Auntie that Gina was going to climb into the bed next to her. She was groggy but responded, "Okay, just don't pee-pee the bed." Gina and I laughed so hard I'm surprised we didn't do just that, as Auntie drifted off to sleep with a smile on her face.

On Thursday morning I don't remember anything particular, except we had another day to be with Auntie. The priest came and said some prayers with us. As the day progressed, Auntie seemed to get closer to the next life and into a decreased level of awareness. Before Gina's husband Steve arrived, Gina started to question why her mother was fighting. She felt Auntie wasn't ready to leave this life. We went to the living room to discuss if we should put her back into the hospital. I listened as she shared her feelings, but this wasn't a decision I could make. I told her what I felt would happen if we put her back into the hospital, and what Auntie had said when she was questioned by the doctor about her wishes, should a problem arise. After our discussion, Gina decided we should continue with what we were doing. The rest of the people Auntie would want to see were coming in the morning. Gina and Steve settled onto the living room floor, and Gina told me to wake her when it was our turn.

The next day Auntie's level of awareness decreased even more than the day before. I talked with Anita that morning; she had spent the night with Grandma, and explained how serious Auntie's condition was. She planned on bringing Grandma out to see Auntie. The changes in Auntie's body continued to bring her closer to the next life and further from ours. We were all gathered in her room as we said our goodbyes, told her we loved her, and we would meet again. As she took her final breaths, we cried and continued to tell her to look for the light and for Grandpa, that he would be waiting for her. I told her I would always be there if Gina needed me. Then Auntie quietly took her soul and left her lifeless body with us.

When everyone left the room, I prepared her body. I felt relief that she was out of the pain but saddened that she was no longer with us. The next day I went to help with the final funeral arrangements. Ironically, Auntie and Gina had gone a month before and prearranged the funeral. On my way home I cried and told the Lord I wished I had asked more about her wishes. I got home and called Michelle and asked about making a tape of songs for the wake. After three to four hours we completed a tape of five songs: "You Light Up My Life," "The Wind Beneath My Wings,' "Through the Years," "You Decorated My Life," and "The Rose."

When I got home, I went to bed exhausted. Early the next morning, the day of the wake, the Lord blessed me with a spiritual experience. Auntie came to me in a dream. When I awoke, I felt we were together.

I said, "Auntie, the Lord allowed you to come back to me." She looked solemn. My guess is she was aware of the pain we felt. I kissed and hugged her and asked my questions as I cried. I awoke sitting straight up in the bed, looking around the room for her. I called Mom and told her about my dream.

At the wake I gave a eulogy and shared my dream. I had asked her if she wanted Gina and Uncle Roger to receive a rose from her. She said yes. I gave them each a rose Mom had purchased for me.

After the eulogy Uncle Roger came up and I reassured him she wanted him to receive a rose. He walked up to the casket and placed the rose on Auntie's body. I said, "Roger, that was your rose from her." He said, "She believed if you prayed and received a rose, your wish would come true."

I don't remember much about the funeral. I read a poem that Aunt Anita gave a friend and said she would like it read at the graveside.

For the first week or two after the funeral, I missed Auntie an awful lot. I kept close contact with Gina. But I never fully grieved Aunt Anita until later. I swept it under the carpet. I had weepy days, but for the most part, I brushed it aside. I began grieving about a year later. I called Colleen and told her how lately it hit me that Aunt Anita was not coming back. The grief I felt was intensified. I guess I didn't work through it completely because when Louie died, I felt the pain of her death once again. This is how I determined that one never escapes the grief; it always catches up with us one way or another.

My life would have been so different without Aunt Anita. She was there for me in so very many ways; we had a special relationship. She was my mentor. I believe one of the reasons I wanted to be a pediatric nurse was to follow in her footsteps and strive to be as good a nurse as she was. She always accepted me for who I was and encouraged me to believe in myself and to use the gifts God has given me. She was a very special woman. I will miss her, but I've learned to tuck her in my heart and keep her there until we are reunited.

The next two experiences I will share involve friends. The first experience was with a friend Sharon whom I had met while going to nursing school. We are still friends, and we see each other on a regular basis. The second was with my very dear friend Colleen, who has been there for me in more ways than I could probably recount.

The day began as any other day, April 20, 1995. I had to do some errands and made tentative lunch plans with Colleen. Sharon called first thing in the morning. I hadn't expected to hear from her, since she had worked twelve-hour night shifts over the weekend. She sounded exhausted and on the brink of tears. She said "I'm not sure how much more I can take. I don't know how you did this with your grandfather." Her grandfather had cancer and apparently had declined rapidly. It is difficult watching someone you love die; you feel so incredibly helpless. I tried my best to console her and offered to come over. She said she'd be all right, and I told her to call if she needed anything.

When we spoke a little while later, she sounded a bit stronger and still felt there was no need for me to come over. I asked for the address just in case. Then I called Mom and told her I felt Sharon needed my physical support but wasn't saying so. Mom and I hadn't finished the conversation when the line beeped. It was Sharon. She had changed her mind and asked if I could come over. I said I would be there as soon as possible. I left a message on Colleen's machine explaining briefly and told her I would call her later.

As I drove to Sharon's grandfather's home, many thoughts were going through my mind—the desire to be there for Sharon and her family, as well as my concern that I only say and do things to ease their pain. I really didn't know her grandfather or her family. When I arrived less than an hour later, Sharon met me on the porch with all the pain, grief, and tears I had seen on Gina's face as well as my own just six months before when Auntie died. We embraced, and I held her as she cried, hoping some of my strength would help her through this.

As we entered the house, I said hello and embraced her family members. Sharon brought me into her grandfather's room. I believe the family followed us in. I did a brief assessment. His blood pressure was low, and his pulse was weak. His respirations were shallow with intermittent apnea episodes. His feet were mottled. (As death is nearing, the skin has the look of lace.) His hands were cool to the touch. (This happens as the circulation begins to slow.) After I finished the assessment, we left the room and Sharon asked how long he had. I said, "Only God knows, but my estimate is about three to six hours."

I must admit I was surprised. I had expected to come and try to ease their pain, give them a break if they needed one, and then head back home. I hadn't actually thought he was so close to dying. I spent time in and out of the room, trying to lend support when I could. I left the room so that the family could be alone with him. About forty-five minutes went by, and little by little the family came out of his room. So I decided to head back in. Sharon's sister was in the room alone. I asked how he was. She said, "No change."

Unbeknown to her there was a big change. He had entered the final stage of dying, and his breathing had changed drastically. I told her it was very close and said it would be a good time to call in any family members who wanted to be with him. She went closer to her grandfather's side, and I went to wake Sharon. Then I called the rest of the family. I stood in the outer part of the doorway and for some reason ended up at the top of the bed. I whispered in his ear to look for the light. Five minutes later, Grandpa had gone home to Jesus. By the end of the afternoon I learned many wonderful things about their grandfather—his kindness and caring for others. The family felt he had chosen this day because it was his deceased wife's birthday. What a wonderful birthday present he had given his wife.

As expected, the next few days were difficult for Sharon and her family. I worked nights, so I called to check on them as often as I could and arranged to work a double Saturday night and Sunday day shift so that I could have Monday off for the funeral. I was very honored when Sharon called and asked me if I would sing at her grandfather's funeral. I told her I didn't think I could.

Singing was a hobby, but I didn't feel I would be able to sing with an organist without the opportunity to rehearse. She sounded so disappointed and said, "But Terri, you have to. I told my family what a nice voice you have, and I really want you to sing." The last thing I wanted to do was disappoint a friend, especially at a time like this.

I went up to church and borrowed the songbook and tried a couple of songs. Then I came up with what I felt would be the perfect solution/compromise. I called Sharon and told her I could do a song for them a cappella either at the Mass or at the graveside. Sharon spoke with her family and the graveside was their choice. I sang "Be Not Afraid," and my knees were shaking so uncontrollably, I was surprised my voice wasn't shaking. With the Lord's help, the song came out better than I could have hoped.

The little miracle of this experience was that before I told Sharon I could sing a cappella, her sister had a dream that someone was singing a cappella at the funeral. For reasons I'm not aware of, it was very important to Sharon's sister to have someone sing. The Lord answers even the smallest of prayers.

Sharing the experience of Sharon's grandfather's death with Sharon and her family has brought us closer, and I'm sure has bonded our friendship into eternity. I was saddened for them at the passing of their loved one, but the grief I felt was related to the pain I knew my friend was experiencing.

I don't fully understand why I was chosen to be with Sharon, her family, and grandfather at the time of his death. It could be simply that I was instrumental in finding Misty, her grandfather's dog, a home. Or maybe I was there to bring them all in the room so that they could be with him at the time of his passing from this life to the next. I was honored to be with them in their time of need. The gratitude they expressed, the comfort they said I was to them is worth more to me than I could express in words. In the spectrum it's not all that important that I understand why I was there. God knows why he wanted me there, and that's good enough for me…

In July 1995 Colleen called and said that Dick, her dad, had inoperable cancer. The doctor told her they could possibly buy him some time by administering chemotherapy and/or radiation. She had taken her dad for more tests, and when she returned to her parents' home, the doctor called and said her dad had two weeks to two months to live. The cancer was found in his lung, abdomen, and in a lesion on the brain. I thought it was inconsiderate that the doctor didn't tell them when they were in the office because it left her with a decision of telling her parents or waiting until their appointment the following week. She was devastated as anyone would be in finding out a parent had only a short time to live. My heart was breaking for her, and "I'm sorry" just didn't cut it. I told her I'd do whatever she needed. Since she had asked my opinion, I told her if the doctors had called her at home, time must truly be a factor. I offered to go with her and lend my support in any way that I could if she chose to tell her parents herself.

She called the next morning to say she decided to go out and tell her parents and asked if I could go with her. I called Mom to pray with me, to help me say words that would only bring comfort while speaking the truth. We left the children with Tony and drove to Colleen's parents'. Colleen handled the heart-wrenching words with sensitivity and warmth. I answered questions to the best of my ability, trying to give areas of importance to think about from my past experiences, so if possible all her dad's wishes could be granted. After we visited for a short time, I kissed "Dad" goodbye. A situation like this brings people close together quickly. I told him I'm always only a phone call away if he needed anything.

Colleen had a heavy load to carry, and I wished I could do something more to ease her pain. I think one of the big differences is that they knew his time was limited so they spent time talking about things that needed to be done. With my own loved ones, I wasn't aware of the final stage until we were in it, and then you don't have the time to think about anything except caring for their immediate needs.

Over the next couple of weeks, while I visited, sometimes Dick felt like talking, so I answered questions the best I could. I had the opportunity to have a brief conversation about relationships with God and how one would only need to ask the Lord for forgiveness for any wrongdoing, that his eternal home in heaven would be open to him. Colleen and I had discussed my speaking to him in this way if the opportunity presented itself.

On August 17, I headed out to the grocery store early. I had taken three of Colleen's children home last evening and wanted to bring a meal when I brought the children back. Unexpectedly, Colleen called and said the hospice nurse was there and felt death could be anytime. She asked me to bring the children, but said not to rush. With Tony's help, I gathered the food and children, and we were out the door in five minutes. I knew in my heart he would wait for his grandchildren, and me.

On the twenty-minute drive I had to say something to the children to prepare them. I can't recall my exact words, but I explained that Grandpa was getting close to the time of leaving this earth and going to his home with Jesus. I asked if they had any questions and answered them to the best of my ability. They wanted to know if he would die today and if he would go to heaven.

Colleen was waiting at the back door. I told her briefly what the children and I had discussed, and she brought the children to see their grandfather while I gathered the food. When she came to get me, I said hello to her mom and went to Dick's side. I whispered, "It's Terri. When you're ready to go home to Jesus, he or a loved one will be waiting for you. Follow the light." I did a quick assessment and left the room. I spoke with the hospice nurse who said she had an errand to do if I would be there. She would return shortly. I told Colleen I didn't think "Dad" would be going home to Jesus immediately. While no one but God knows how long, from my previous experiences, my estimate was a couple of hours.

I went outside to sit; Colleen and her brother were sitting out there also. She mentioned to her brother that I thought it might be a couple of hours and asked if he had gone in the room yet. He said no. I asked him if I could ask a question. He said, yes. I asked why he hadn't been in to see his dad, and he responded, "I'm not sure." I explained that I understood how difficult this is, but that if he had anything he wanted to say to his dad, now was a good time. Even though his dad might not be able to respond to him in the manner he was used to, he could still hear what was being said. When Colleen was ready to go back into the room, I followed, suggesting it might be a good time to bring her grandmother in.

Much to my surprise, Colleen's brother was sitting on the bed, stroking his dad's hand. My heart felt as if it was breaking for many reasons. Colleen's grandma kept looking at me and asked me if I could do anything to help him. She knew I was a nurse and couldn't understand why I was just standing there. It was too difficult for her to understand that I was doing what I felt the Lord wanted me to do to help Dick with his passage from this life to the next and to ease the family's pain if at all possible.

I asked Colleen if anyone would object to some prayers. I said prayers from the heart, asking our Lord to guide Dick's way home. He had been pretty still before and during the prayers, and when I told him to look for the light, he squinted his eyes. As I was stroking his hair, he reached above his head, grabbed my hand, and brought it to his side. We finished our prayers and sat silently for a while. After a short period of time, Dick seemed anxious, making noises and pulling his hands up and away. When the hospice nurse returned, we spoke about this, and she shared that sometimes too much stimulation has a way of almost holding the person to this world, when they are trying to go on to the next. I mentioned this to Colleen and suggested that if only two went in at a time, maybe it would ease his anxiousness.

Everyone took turns spending time alone with Dick. Colleen and I were sitting with her grandma when her sister-in-law came out of the room and stated, "He seems to be having a very hard time breathing." As we went into the room, he was very near to his new beginning, and I told Colleen it would be a good idea to have anyone who wanted to be in the room to come in now. As close as Colleen and I are, as her father's passing came nearer, I felt awkward; I wasn't sure what my place was. I started toward the door, but for some reason I didn't leave. Instead, I began praying silently and reminded the family he could hear them if they wanted to say anything.

With tears in our eyes, we said our goodbyes until we meet again, as Dick softly took his last breath and continued his journey home to Jesus. I prepared the body, waited for the men from the funeral home, and stayed a little longer before I headed for home. It had been an emotional day for everyone.

Three days later we attended the memorial service and burial and then went back to the house for a small gathering. The tension had eased on everyone's faces, but not the sorrow. It will take a long time, before the sharp pain feels more like a dull ache, and the memories come back and bring a smile to one's face.

While Colleen and I have been close friends for a long time, this experience cemented our relationship. I came to love her father during that month, and a bond developed between us. It was an honor to have been with him during this time. I felt grief and mourned his death, but much of the grief I felt was because of the pain my dear friend was experiencing. I felt at a loss, not knowing what to say or do. I have learned since Louie's death, there really were no words I could have said to take her pain away. What I did say, "I love you, and I'm here if you need me," hopefully eased some of the pain.

From the experiences I have shared with you, I hope that you can see how different relationships will bring different journeys of grief. Grandma Toon was in her seventies, had no fear of dying, and was ready to die. She had a near-death experience at age seventeen and had visions of our Lord more than once. She was a very important person in our lives, a role model of a true Christian woman. Caring for her was only a small way I could show my love and gratitude for all she had blessed us with. There was difficulty in letting her go; it was my selfishness that wanted her here. Thirteen years later, I still miss her. My heart has healed, and my love for her remains constant until we will be together again.

With Grandpa, the pain was simply the fact that he was not

here any longer. He added so very much to our lives, and living across from him my entire childhood, I got used to having him around. The thought of his dying really didn't cross my mind until he became ill. But what more could we have asked from the Lord? He had lived for a month shy of ninety-eight years. He was sharp as a tack until the very end, especially when he played pinochle and checkers. He still cooked and kept a huge garden in his backyard in the summers. I miss the taste of his fresh vegetables. He said his secret was the rainwater he collected in that big barrel in the back yard and watered his garden with tender loving care. I was blessed to have had him for my grandfather. My heart has healed, and being reunited with him will once again fill my heart with joy.

You will remember that my journey with Aunt Anita had continued for a very long time and in many respects continues today; I never took the time to grieve her passing. I miss her. My heart aches at times for her because I know how much joy she would have felt being with her grandchildren. I can't say that my heart has fully mended from her death. I believe I will have to continue to work on that aspect on this journey of grief. But for the most part I treasure all the good memories, which help while I work toward healing. She was in her early sixties, and if the cancer had stayed in remission, she could have been with us today. I realize now if that was part of God's plan, the cancer would not have returned, so he must have something else in mind for her or felt her work on this earth was complete.

The other two journeys were different in many respects. With not having really known Sharon's grandfather, everything I was feeling was related to the difficulty Sharon was having. My sorrow wasn't really grief; it was caused from the obvious pain on their faces and my hope to ease some of that pain. I will look forward to getting to know her grandfather someday in heaven.

I did mourn the loss of Colleen's dad, for when you have a connection with someone and bond so quickly as we did, you feel the initial emptiness. I don't believe the emptiness lasted as long as it normally would because the bond wasn't there long. I do think of him and am glad he was a part of my life, if only for a brief time. My emptiness changed to grief because of my overwhelming concern for Colleen and the pain I could see on her face. She and her dad were very close, and I knew this was going to be a big void in her life. I did what I could to help ease her pain, but as we all know, we must work through the grief in our own time and with the strength we find in ourselves and in the strength the Lord gives us. When it is my time, I will welcome seeing her dad in our eternal home.

About the Author

Theresa, known as Terri to her friends, has lived in Ohio all of her life. She enjoys the changing of the seasons; however, winter is not her favorite time. But she associates the thaw of winter and the changing to spring with the warming and blossoming of flowers, trees coming to life, and the warmth of the brown grass changing to green with an individual's progression through the grief process.

She has been married to Tony, the love of her life, for twenty years. God has blessed them with two sons, who have added precious moments to their lives.

Theresa had never anticipated writing a book, least of all about grief. She hopes that the feelings, emotions, and thoughts shared in this book will help you to find a new beginning to healing as you progress through your journey.

NOTES